AN END TO NIGHTTIME OVEREATING

Your 10-Day Definitive Guide to Nailing 'Pigula' (Your Nighttime Overeating Vampire) in Its Coffin Forever!

Glenn Livingston Ph.D.

Yoav Ezer

DISCLAIMER: For education only. You are responsible for determining your own nutritional, medical, and psychological needs. If you require assistance with this task you must consult with a licensed physician, nutritionist, psychologist, and/or other professional. No medical, psychological, and/or nutritional advice is offered through this book. Even though the author is a licensed psychologist, he does not offer psychological services, psychological advice and/or psychological counsel in his role as author of this book. In particular, if you have ever been diagnosed with an eating disorder you agree not to create your Food Plan and/or any Food Rules and/or to change your diet in any way without the input and approval of a psychiatrist, psychologist, and licensed dietician. Psy Tech Inc. and/or Never Ever Again, Inc. is only willing to license you the right to utilize this book in the event you agree with these terms. If you do not agree with these terms, please do not read the book, delete it from all electronic devices you own, and/or return it to your place of purchase for a full refund (where applicable). Last, if you follow a link in this book and purchase something on the website on which you land, Psy Tech Inc., and/or Never Ever Again, Inc. may be compensated. While we will never recommend anything we believe is anything other than stellar for your own education and wellbeing, we do not have a neutral position, so you are advised to do your own due diligence before purchase.

Further, although the legend of vampires, werewolves, zombies, demons, and other mythological creatures may be discussed in this book, Psy Tech, its principals, and employees actively discourage biting other people, drinking blood, drawing blood without an appropriate medical license, driving stakes through human bodies whether living, 'undead', or other; donating blood to persons who claim to be vampires, biting other people, allowing other people to bite you, and/or otherwise engaging in activities considered to be unsafe, harmful to self and/or others, unethical, and/or immoral. Many activities associated with vampires, vampire hunters, and vampire slayers are dangerous, unsanitary, and illegal.[Y1] *Despite making every effort to be objective in presenting the facts about vampires, zombies, werewolves, demons, and other legends within this book, our personal view is that they are NOT real but rather a fascinating metaphor, the study of which provides tremendous entertainment, insight into the human mind, knowledge of a wide diversity of cultures and peoples from around the world. More importantly, it provides a powerful metaphor you can use to help you stop overeating at night and that is the ONLY application we recommend.*

Also, by reading this book you agree to be solely responsible for what food, drink, and/or supplements you choose to put in your mouth. We have no way of knowing your unique biochemistry, medical conditions, and/or food sensitivities.

Finally, the term "Pigula™" is not intended to represent anyone with the last name Pigula, but rather refers to all thoughts, feelings, images, and impulses which sug-

gest that a person overeats between the moment dinner ends and breakfast begins the next day. Any similarities to those persons with the last name Pigula are unintentional.

INTRODUCTION AND HOW TO USE THIS BOOK

This book contains a comprehensive solution to the nighttime eating problem, geared (mostly) towards those who consider night indulgence a serious and persistent issue, not necessarily those who only eat a few extra cookies on occasion in the evening. That said, you can apply the protocol to help with *any* level of night eating problem, provided you are awake when the problem occurs. It may also be helpful for people who eat in their sleep—*for example those who wake up surprised to find crumbs on their pillow*—but we have yet to collect enough evidence to support this.

This solution is based on the "Never Binge Again" (NBA) methodology first introduced by Dr. Livingston in his 2015 book of the same name. In the four years since its publication, Never Binge Again has amassed over 500,000 readers and helped thousands of people to stop overeating, resume a normal relationship with food, and in many cases, lose weight.

While the system presented in this book relies on the Never Binge Again method, it has been aggressively tailored for the nighttime eating problem and contains specific step-by-step instructions towards that end. If you haven't read NBA you are welcome to do so, but please rest assured this is *not* required. If you *have* read NBA, you'll undoubtedly find *some* concepts repeated. However, the vampire analogies and specific instructions presented herein have been significantly customized to address nighttime overeating, and spaced repetition is very beneficial to applying any subject in broader context. Regardless of your previous experience with Never Binge Again, we therefore recommend you read this book in its entirety.

Also, it's best to first read this book one time all the way through to acquaint yourself with the system it describes. Only after doing so should you actually execute the protocol presented in chapters 5 to 9, creating and solidifying your own set of personal rules to help end your nighttime overeating habit.

We hope you'll enjoy this book. More importantly, we hope you realize it can still end your nighttime overeating problem. We took immense pleasure in writing it!

CHAPTER 1: RESISTING THE LURE OF NIGHT TIME EATING

Kicking the Nighttime Eating Habit in 10 Days

Have you ever been in a truly dark place? It's hard to find anywhere in today's halogen-lit world which really is utterly devoid of light. It's the kind of pitch blackness you find deep in the wilderness on a cloudy, moonless night. Or maybe you experienced utter darkness in the woods, with a thick, impervious canopy above you, after the embers of your fire died.

Were you scared in the darkness? What frightened you? Maybe it was the fear of animals. Or perhaps it was the claustrophobic feeling of the velvety blackness closing in on you which terrified you. Maybe you were scared because you knew that underneath this comfortable, protective, dark cover you were invisible, and you began to wonder what a person might get away with in a gloom so dark that there would be no witnesses.

If you've ever sat in the darkness wondering what depths a human might sink to when they were assured no one else would witness their actions, then you've touched the true nature of your nighttime overeating vampire, "Pigula™!"

When it comes to food, you know what Pigula can "make" you do when nobody is watching, don't you? After all, if you purchased this book, you've probably done things with food at night you wouldn't want ANYONE else to see.

It's OK, according to our national survey more than half the population struggles with overeating at night. It's whether we allow Pigula to become our master vs. make it our slave that counts. Will we dominate it, or allow it to "roam the countryside" at night in search of prey? And what will be the consequences of that decision on our weight, our health, our loved ones...even our immortal soul?

Pigula™ is the special name we have for the inner mental monster that beckons us to gorge *at night*, previously dubbed "The Pig" in Dr. Livingston's bestselling book "Never Binge Again"—*2,000+ reviews and 600,000+ readers - available FREE at www.NeverBingeAgain.com*. This name is more than apt because Pigula's motives, character, and seemingly irresistible allure all parallel the vampires of lore. And just like Dracula, Pigula can either dominate you and make you do unspeakable things, or you can fight it and lock it in its coffin forever – the choice is yours!

Pause for a moment here to take a few deep breaths and consider the following as seriously as you've ever considered anything:

How much better would your life be if you COULD stop overeating at night?

We're NOT talking about occasionally "being good" when you're "on a diet." We want you to imagine nailing Pigula's coffin completely shut forever. What would it be like to be 100% confident you were utterly DONE with nighttime overeating?

That seems impossible from where you sit right now, right?

Indulge us anyway.

See yourself in the mirror 365 days from this very moment, having not broken your diet even once in the evening. You truly conquered nighttime overeating.

What's different? How much weight will you have lost? How much more energy will you have? How much more confident will you feel if you didn't keep giving into those "irresistible" urges? How much more peaceful will your daily state of mind be? What about your relationships with friends, family, and colleagues? What could you wear that you can't wear now? How much more might you enjoy socializing and connecting with others? What else will you have accomplished in your life by then if you simply didn't overeat at night for a full year?

Regardless of how difficult it may be to imagine, we promise by the time you're done reading this book you'll be confident it's possible, because there IS a solution. A special, step by step code we derived from the experience of hundreds of successful readers and clients from around the world. These clients have used the steps described in this book to completely vanquish Pigula and nail its coffin shut forever. These steps are also backed by empirical evidence in a national survey we ourselves commissioned using a representative sample of the United States population, as well as a steadily mounting collection of research studies.

You do NOT have to spend a lifetime at the mercy of these nighttime urges or continue to ruin your health after working so hard to stay on track all day.

We know, we know...

Your Pigula must be screaming now...

The foul creature says it can't be done, there's no method strong enough, and you should put down this stupid book right now. It says "just go get us some junk *('Pigula Slop™')* we can go to town on tonight!" Moreover, when we finish showing you the process, Pigula will say the answer can't possibly be that easy or else you would've done it already: "Glenn and Yoav are complete charlatans and you've wasted your money yet again on another foolish attempt to stop!"

See, Pigula does NOT want to be nailed in its coffin. It wants to hunt at night, like any self-respecting vampire, and like you've been letting it do all these years. It's terrified you might actually learn something which will end the madness. So, Pigula will pull out ALL the stops to get you to dismiss this solution before you give it ANY serious consideration or effort.

It can be very difficult to completely dismiss Pigula at first because it is the embodiment of the unhealthy habits, Pavlovian reactions, and self-defeating thought patterns YEARS *(OFTEN DECADES)* of bad eating and coping with stress have created. So Pigula can't be easily nailed in its coffin without some significant thinking, planning, and effort.

That said, please know that if you are indeed a human being, you are neurologically wired to be superior to Pigula, which derives from the more primitive, lower parts of your brain. You ARE perfectly capable of installing and acting upon an alternative behavioral plan when the nighttime overeating urge hits. We know this for certain because we've done it ourselves, and because we've talked to so many successful people who previously felt hopeless to fix the problem—at least as hopeless as you may feel now, we promise.

And you can do it in just 10 days!

Who Are We?

Dr. Glenn Livingston

I'm a formerly obese guy with very poor cardiovascular genetics...

A guy who almost ate himself to death despite a dozen warnings from doctors and other health professionals...

Who wasted years of his life believing he had a mysterious disease which caused him to compulsively overeat...

And who used to think he was powerless to resist bagels, pizza, chocolate, donuts, pasta, potato chips, and pretty much anything else which tasted good in mass quantities.

My ongoing food compulsions and preoccupations did not deter me, however, from earning a Ph.D. in clinical psychology, nor from building a large, very successful practice, nor even from funding my own food-preference research project with 40,000+ people.

And for over 25 years I was the CEO of companies which provided tens of millions of dollars in research and consulting services to Fortune 500 firms including major food manufacturers like Lipton, Kraft, Nabisco, etc.

Frankly, I'm a guy who couldn't stop thinking about food, even while he was working with psychotherapy patients and coaching clients...

Someone who spent most of his life feeling desperate to control his food problem. That is, until I discovered a child-like trick of mind which got me thinking like a permanently thin person...

A weird idea which got in my head and grew progressively

stronger by itself, no matter how hard my fat-thinking-self tried to eliminate it!

Yoav Ezer

I'm a formerly obese guy who was dominated by Pigula for decades.

And despite having a successful army career followed by two stints as CEO in software companies who sold over $5,000,000 worth of products and services, couldn't prevent Pigula from getting himself to a record weight of 252 pounds at 5'8''.

I'm the guy that waited exactly 5 minutes after his wife went to bed to sneak to the fridge and start the nightly "party".

The guy who wouldn't be satisfied until he's had something sweet, then a lot of salty and fatty stuff, followed by a lot of sweet things for dessert.

The guy who used to throw out the garbage at night just so his wife wouldn't notice the slew of packages and boxes that were "mysteriously" added to the trash (who was I kidding?)

I'm the guy who would buy two cakes on Friday, one for the family for the weekend, and one for himself for Friday night.

I'm also the guy who completely stopped bingeing at night and haven't had a nightly binge for 3 years.

I've also lost 90 pounds on the way and helped Glenn spread the word about Never Binge Again to hundreds of thousands of people across the world.

And I'm the CEO of Never Ever Again *(Glenn's and my company).*

I would love to help you kick this nasty nightly eating habit in the shins!

Let's go!!!

How Big (And How Serious) is the Nighttime Overeating Problem?

The impulse to overeat in the evening *feels* irresistible to hundreds of millions of people worldwide. When we commissioned our own nighttime eating survey with a representative sample of the United States population, we found 57.5% of respondents reported eating more than they planned to at night.

The fact that the majority of America overeats at night was NOT, however, the most disturbing finding. Unfortunately, we also found nighttime overeaters:

> ➢ **Have more than *twice* as much weight to lose!** *(230% more than those who don't eat more than they planned to in the evening)...*
>
> ➢ **Are more than *three times* as likely to need to lose at least fifty pounds!** *(348% more)...*
>
> ➢ **Are *less than half* as likely to be at their ideal weight!** *(47.2% as likely)...*

Worse yet, many *(if not most)* of our clients and readers feel absolutely panicked about the problem. They seem to have developed the belief there's something different about them which other people are simply incapable of understanding. Something genetic. Or maybe they've dug such a deep behavioral groove in their nighttime eating brain that there's just no going back.

Unfortunately, this is a source of suffering beyond measure. It's extremely demoralizing, can ruin your health, and create perpetual insecurity about ever being able to permanently lose weight or accomplish other fitness goals. For many, it also ruins their ability to participate in other important areas of life, stealing the energy they need to enjoy their children, family, nature, etc.

Without the formula in this book they began to believe they were doomed. After all, Pigula's Whispers ARE eerily convincing:

> "There's just got to be something for YOU today, You're under so much stress, you deserve a treat. It'll be so tasty AND RELAXING" ...
>
> "Watching TV and eating is really the only thing you enjoy... go for it!"
>
> "You did so well today. You deserve to celebrate!"
>
> "You won't be able to sleep if you don't eat more" ...
>
> "Everyone has their own vice. Some do drugs, some are sex addicts, you just love food. That's perfectly ok..."

...and a myriad of other falsehoods which SEEM 100% true at the time you hear them.

Plus... there's another "small" problem...

It's Almost Impossible to Stop Dangerous Eating Habits By "Loving Yourself" More

Identifying and locking your nighttime-feasting alter-ego away is THE key to de-programming this soul-destroying habit. By giving a voice to this utterly compelling urge to eat you can control it and weaken it every day, until the once all-powerful compulsion disappears entirely.

Inevitably when people begin to give their inner-eating compulsion a voice, they realize they'll need to get very tough with it to overcome it... at least during the first 30 days.

Most people spend their entire lives trying to avoid being tough, controlling and/or angry. In modern society we are taught these emotions have no place, that we mustn't treat our peers, friends or family in this way. We are also taught we can't treat *ourselves* this way either. Thus, most people believe they will cause themselves irreparable harm if they treat any part of themselves with anger or contempt.

But here's the thing...

The part of ourselves we need to exert control over is not what we consider to be our human self. It is, instead, the most animalistic part of our psyche.

Imagine your job forced you to travel out of the country for an entire year, and while you were gone you left your house and your beloved dog in the care of a relative you thought you could trust. When you got back, however, you discovered you couldn't have been more wrong...

He let your dog piss all over the house and snatch food off the table. He allowed it to walk into the cupboard, tear open bags, and eat whatever and as much as it wanted.

Now, a year later, the dog is almost feral *(and very fat).*

Upon your return, you try to restore order, but the dog snarls and barks at you when you try to take away its food or lock the cupboard.

Would you hug it and give it a treat every time it misbehaved?

Of course, you wouldn't, because that would only reinforce the feral behavior.

Because you dearly love your dog, you'd reassert your superiority and re-train it. The alternatives, after all, would be to let it continue dominating your household, or to have it put down. Both are unacceptable.

Your nighttime eating alter-ago is your feral inner dog. You must ruthlessly train and dominate it or life together will become untenable.

Plus, nighttime overeaters are often quite angry and ashamed of years struggling to control this harmful behavior. What if asserting your superiority over these urges was the one thing that could finally allow you to stop being angry at *(and/or ashamed of)* yourself, thereby raising, not lowering your self-esteem.

Now, because your inner-monster overeats *at night,* we shall call it "Pigula", and it will hereafter house ALL your nighttime-overeating thoughts.

Sun Tzu the famous Chinese general said, "If you know the enemy and know yourself, you need not fear the result of a hundred battles." Therefore, before we approach nailing Pigula in its coffin forever, let's get to know it a little better!

CHAPTER 2: WHAT IS THE NIGHTTIME EATING VAMPIRE? (PIGULA)

First off, the most important thing to remember about Pigula is that it is not you!

Please bear with us a few minutes and imagine you've just met a wise, powerful old wizard. This wizard knows the secret to stopping nighttime eating and he is here to help you...

"First" he says,

"I'm going to draw out your HIGHER SELF"

And as he waves his wand and casts his ancient magic, he transfers all your positive, loving, empowering thoughts into a bright, human-like silhouette on your right...

You can see all your dreams, aspirations and plans being drawn into it.

You can see all the joys you've experienced *(and are yet to experience)* in this silhouette.

You can see the care you have for your health, your body, and your well-being.

You can see it filled with all the happiness of which you are capable.

Your silhouette is filled with music, compassion, and the will to learn and laugh.

It is filled with confidence.

It is full of love for your friends and family *(and even strangers)...*

And the desire to be there and support them as best as you can for as long as possible.

But most importantly...

Your silhouette is brimming with the determination to live your life to the fullest!

"Now" Says the wizard...

"I'm going to draw PIGULA out"

Suddenly his incantation changes, it becomes menacing and primal.

And all your negative, harmful, angry and shameful thoughts and behaviors are drawn in black wisps of smoke into a dark, ominous presence on your left...

This second presence stands in sharp contrast to the first silhouette...

For Pigula is filled with an overpowering urge to eat at night.

It lusts only for its junk.

It will say and do whatever it takes to have its nighttime junk food orgy, no matter the cost to your personal health, happiness, and wellbeing.

It will try to make you feel shame!

It will try to intensify feelings of stress and loneliness.

It will attempt to make you feel so bored that you THINK you have no option but to feed it what it wants.

It will not hesitate for a minute to say you are terminally fat, and there is nothing you can do to improve. It wants you to think nothing will fix this problem, no matter what you try, because it knows if you'll feel insecure and anxious enough, it can get you to say "screw it, might as accept my fate and just eat, eat, eat!"

See, Pigula is absolutely ruthless. It will say absolutely ANYTHING to get you to open the fridge and stuff your face.

It will pretend to be your friend, but it really doesn't care about you at all.

It will say it wants you to feel happy. That food is the only thing that can help.

It's LYING!

"Now" Says the wizard,

"Do you want to see how this works?"

"Yes" You respond!

"OK..." He says,

And with a wave of his wand he materializes a pint of ice-cream in-front of you.

"Now listen to Pigula and do as he says"

And as you focus your attention on Pigula, you begin to hear a voice. The more you listen, the more powerful and luring the voice becomes....

"Eat the ice-cream! You'll feel a lot better" The voice says.

"You'll finally be able to relax" it continues.

And, unfortunately, as the wizard instructed, you take a tub of ice-cream and eat.

As soon as you finish eating, Pigula grows. It becomes more solid and the dark fog around it intensifies.

To your horror, Pigula strikes the shiny silhouette, your higher-self, with one of its claws and creates a very visible dent in a white, shiny wisp of smoke that contains every dream you've had ever since you were a child. Then, with another two quick slashes, it cuts out a swath of your health and happiness which dissipate into thin air.

Seeing this makes you sick to your gut, but then Pigula turns to you and says...

"Don't worry! Wasn't the ice-cream great? We deserved this treat today! Tomorrow we'll get back on track and everything will be ok"

And his sweet, luring voice sooths your horror immediately.

You forget about your health and happiness. You forget about your goals and dreams. All that left is a twinge of guilt.

"Now" Says Pigula.

"Since we already blew our diet for today, why not have a little cake too?"

And a delicious looking chocolate-cake materializes before you.

"It's really going to be fun!!!" Pigula Whispers...

"ENOUGH!!!!" – The wizard's booming voice penetrates the fog Pigula's words has engulfed you with.

"Now, behold what happens when you do NOT listen to Pigula" says the wizard.

"The next time you hear Pigula's voice instructing you to eat, REFUSE. No matter how compelling its whispers may sound, do NOT give in!"

And sure enough, the second the wizard steps back, you can hear Pigula whispering once again...

"How about it? Let's eat the cake!"

"No!" you say

For a second, Pigula looks perplexed. It is unaccustomed to being defied, but it quickly rebounds...

"Why not, you really want to eat this cake!?"

And as it utters those words, an overwhelming urge washes over you. You feel you have to eat the cake. In fact, it FEELS for the moment that life has no meaning without the darn cake.

But as the wizard instructed, you resist!

"NO!" you say...

And for the next 30 minutes you battle it out. Pigula uses its entire arsenal. It throws every semi-logical justification, every emotional urge, and every physical desire it can at you. But you simply drink a glass of water, move around a bit, and find yourself able to resist its powers.

And as you feel the urges dissipate, something amazing happens.

Pigula shrinks a little.

And at the same time your higher self grows and shines brighter!

You can see your confidence grow.

You can see your health and well-being shine brighter within it.

You can see one of your dreams morphing into a plan before your eyes.

"And that my young disciple" Says the wizard, who's been silent up until now, "is the trick".

He waves his wand and a book appears.

"Inside this book, lays a simple, but powerful spell you can use to shrink Pigula until it is but a mere shadow. Then you may lock it in its coffin forever."

"This book is yours" He says and gives you the book.

"You've already learned the first step in the process, to separate Pigula from yourself."

"Now read the book and apply the rest of the step by step instructions it contains. Do this and you WILL vanquish Pigula and live your life to the fullest."

Sound good? Then keep reading, because you already have the foundational insight...

PIGULA IS NOT YOU!

Well done!

You've learned the first step... to separate Pigula from yourself.

As crazy as it sounds, you must learn to treat Pigula with the same distaste and disrespect you'd feel for a BULLY. Because every time you party with food at night despite your best-laid plans, there's actually a little voice inside you — *Pigula's voice* — working hard to make it "OK". And Pigula (the Bully) doesn't care how sick it makes you, how much pain it causes, and/or how much it derails your best laid plans to achieve important goals.

All Pigula cares about is convincing you it is perfectly OK to eat a whole LOT of garbage...

But it's NOT OK! And this trick of mind is how you finally get fed up with the internal thoughts which—until now— have been ruining so much of your life in exchange for a few moments of late-night toxic pleasure.

For this reason, we're going to voluntarily and aggressively separate ourselves from Pigula in our own mental space, and in so doing we're going to gain 100% dominance over its destructive ideas.

Pigula is NOT you and deserves NO respect. Learn to hear its Whispers, then promptly ignore them.

Is Pigula Real?

Of course not!

We don't believe there's a REAL vampire inside anyone.

It's only a mental concept. A voluntary trick of mind.

But here's the thing: It's not "just" a trick of mind, it's THE trick of mind that works where others fail!

We may wish to acknowledge it is a trick in order to maintain our sanity. However, in order to get the job done, once we've acknowledged this, it becomes imperative to treat Pigula as if it were real.

In fact, in order for the trick to work, it has to seem 100% real to us.

You might struggle with this idea at first. Pigula would certainly prefer you believed it didn't exist. Because then you'd think its Whispers were your own thoughts — and, as you'll soon discover, this is the ONLY way Pigula can get you to feed it.

REMEMBER: It's your mind and you're allowed to organize your thoughts and feelings any way you want. Pigula exists because you SAY it exists, end of story.

> "Are you really taking any of this nonsense seriously? C'mon... let's just have our regular night-food party, relax and forget about this nonsense!"
>
> Sincerely – Pigula

Five Reasons why it's extremely difficult to naturally control Pigula without aggressively separating yourself from and dominating it. *(Why trying to "love yourself thin" and/or "fill the hole in your heart so you won't keep filling*

the hole in your stomach" almost always fails.)

The first reason stems from the way our brains are structured.

See, our brains evolved in distinct parts. *(And yes, we're dramatically oversimplifying for illustration) ...*

The oldest part is the Brain Stem (**The Lizard Brain**), it is the seat of our most animalistic instincts. The instincts that govern eating, breeding and fighting originate from this part of our brain.

It is a very powerful, but very simple part of our brain, and it's where Pigula reigns supreme. This is the seat of emergency responses like "feast and famine" and "fight or flight." That is why the urge to eat is so powerful... it's perceived as an emergency.

But luckily, evolution provided us with an even stronger neurobiological component – the Frontal Lobe. This is where our higher-self lives, where logical thinking and long-term plans are empowered. Without a Frontal Lobe love, philosophy, and everything else we call human could not exist...

That's because the frontal lobe is able to override impulses and decisions the Lizard brain throws at us.

This is evident, because we don't try to copulate with every attractive person we see on the street, and we don't kill or maim every person that angers us.

Societal norms and laws present a punishment that is much greater than the reward we would get if we acted mindlessly on our sexual desires and/or our aggression, and because of this we have learned to inhibit the Lizard Brain's impulses almost without effort.

But as you'll see in a few minutes, our society unfortunately does very little to punish mindless eating. In fact, it encourages it, which is a big part of why the eating instinct in our collective brain is in a constant state of over-performance: 70% of the US population is overweight and 57% of the adult population overeats at night!

But the problem gets worse because our brains are very much geared to create habits or behavioral shortcuts. Generally speaking, this is a good thing because, in our natural environment—*the one we evolved to live in*—habits make our life a lot easier. They allow us to relegate a lot of the hard work to the 'automatic' part of our brain. Thanks to habits, tying our shoes, driving, and a whole slew of other critical activities can be performed semi-automatically. This preserves our precious brain power for more difficult, complicated, or newer tasks.

Unfortunately, it's entirely possible to install bad habits too, and it becomes just as hard to resist executing them as with good habits.

This is particularly true with nighttime eating...

Once you've given yourself a huge yummy reward at night, every day for years or even decades, your mind becomes primed to receive that reward at this given time.

In fact, the nighttime overeating urge eventually begins appearing on its own, without the need for any external trigger. It doesn't matter if you had a good day at work or it if you were loved and adored by your friends and family. It doesn't matter if you were happy with yourself all day long, or extremely self-critical and depressed. Once the lights go out, or perhaps just when your spouse and children are finally asleep, the desire to eat manifests with all its might...

The same way dogs in the famous Pavlovian experiment started salivating when they heard a bell ring.

Which brings us to reason #2 we need to tackle our food prob-

lems with a much more aggressive approach...

There's a FIVE TRILLION-dollar industry that makes a profit every time you let Pigula control your actions. Some fat cat in a white suit with a mustache who laughs all the way to the bank every time you bury your head in a bag, box, or container at night.

You see, the food industry is mind-bendingly big and powerful, and it unfortunately depends on you opening your wallet and buying as much food as you can for your nightly parties.

Today's products are packed with sugar, fat, and other components designed to trigger a pleasure response in our brains. They are also, in many cases, devoid of the nutrients which make us feel full and content. When you eat them, you experience a short burst of pleasure, followed by the hollow feeling that you are still hungry.

This is all by design. It simply makes economic sense for the food industry to help Pigula by creating foods that hit your bliss point without giving you enough nutrition to feel satisfied. That's how you engineer maximum addictive potential into a "food."

Then, of course, Big Advertising (force #3) spends billions to convince us these food-like-substances are irresistible *(and even good for us)*. Food advertising is so powerful and pervasive that it's been able to infiltrate almost every facet of our lives. We eat and/or drink to celebrate just about EVERY occasion: Birthdays, holidays, promotions, births, etc. For Pete's sake, we even celebrate the workday ending with drinking and eating.

Over the last few decades, the advertising industry, funded by an almost unlimited budget from the food industry, has made over-eating into the norm. While acting mindlessly on your sexual desires and aggressive impulses were a big NO-NO, mindlessly eating has been ceremoniously integrated into the very fabric of our culture.

Then, the Addiction Treatment Industry ***(force #4)*** tells us we're "powerless" over our addictions. They say overeaters have a chronic, progressive, mysterious disease against which there is often no human defense. The best we can ever hope for is to abstain one day at a time. This message is readily absorbed by our culture to the point many of us believe we CAN'T give up our pleasure buttons even if we want to!

And finally, the modern employment environment (force #5) is designed to keep employees' "unproductive" activities to a minimum while they are on company time. Which means that the faster you consume your food, the better. So, most employees will go out for a quick bite or eat at their desk. They consume calorie-dense, low nutrition food which allows them to eat quickly and get a boost of energy. They also consume caffeine to squeeze the maximum possible amount of willpower and focus out of themselves on the job.

This leaves people exhausted and deprived of nutrition by the time they reach home at night.

On top of that, taking time to "destress" during workhours is frowned upon, so employees also build up a great deal of tension they subsequently need to release at night.

The combination of stress, stimulants, and low nutrition/high carb foods *(junk food/restaurant food)* results in a very high physical and mental tension level in the evening.

Summarizing...

Big Food puts as much starch, sugar, oil, sodium, fat, excitotoxins, and other chemical stimulants into a small space as they legally can...

Then they package it up to APPEAR healthy and irresistible...

Big Advertising makes us believe it...

Big Addiction Treatment says we're powerless to resist...

And the modern work-place builds up stress, and squeezes all our focus and willpower out of us while leaving us just enough time to consume the low-nutrition, high carb foods Big Food keeps in front of us—while frowning upon any attempts to de-stress on company time.

Then we walk around thinking we're just supposed to love ourselves more when the nightly irresistible cravings appear from the depths of our habitually trained lizard brain!

Is it any wonder almost 60% of the population overeats at night? That we've got a worldwide obesity epidemic on our hands?

But there's very good news...

You CAN set yourself apart from all this with a simple set of techniques. You only need to learn to recognize Pigula's voice when it Whispers, then summarily ignore it, while ensuring you're getting more than enough healthy nutrition throughout the day.

CHAPTER 3: LOCKING PIGULA AWAY IN ITS COFFIN

How Pigula Repeatedly Gets You to Overeat at Night

In the 1931 movie "Dracula", the dreaded vampire, played by the fabulous Bela Lugosi, uses his powers of mind control to make almost every character in the movie bow to his will.

For example, he turns Renfield, the real estate agent, into his slave. Renfield then buys an old Abbey for the Count and makes sure he is safely transported from his home in Transylvania to England. Upon Dracula's arrival, the vampire embarks on a bloody nighttime bingeing campaign consisting of beautiful (sweet) young women. Whenever someone opposes him, Dracula uses his powers to control their minds. Then he either kills or eats them, or both.

The turning point in the movie occurs when Dracula meets Dr. Van Helsing. When Van Helsing exposes Dracula, the Count tries to use his mind control ability dull the Doctor's senses so he can kill him, but the doctor's will is too strong, and Van Helsing is able to awaken from Dracula's trance and use a silver cross to drive Dracula away.

From that point on, the vampire is on the run. He fails in his attempt to make the heroine (Nina) into a vampire. In the end, Van Helsing finds Dracula in his coffin and drives a stake through his heart.

To vanquish Pigula you must be able to do what Dr. Van Helsing did...

To snap out of your food trance and see that it is actually Pigula whispering in your ear...

NOT your own desires being served.

It is Pigula saying...

"You are really hungry!"

"You deserve a reward"

"There's cake in the fridge and no one will know you ate it"

"You REALLY REALLY want it"

Here's how you become your own Dr. Van Helsing...

First of all,...

Remember: You do not have cravings – Pigula does! So, when you feel one coming on, just say:

"I WILL NEVER EAT PIGULA SLOP AGAIN!"

Here are a few key points you need to be aware of so that you can successfully lock Pigula away for good:

Eating even a single bite outside of your evening Food Plan constitutes a nighttime binge – but not because of the calories you consume *(one single bite does not contain that many calories and isn't harmful to your diet).* The reason why taking that one bite is so harmful is because it strengthens Pigula! When you surrender control of your body to Pigula and eat off-plan because of a nighttime urge, even if it's only ONE bite, you strengthen Pigula *(the habit of nighttime eating itself).* But when you resist the urge, when you do not reward it with food, then you begin to extinguish the nighttime eating pattern, and in an amount of time WAY shorter than most people think, the urge becomes much, much weaker. In fact, it can take as little as 10 days to feel completely recovered from nighttime overeating, and rarely does it take more than one month.

So... whenever the urge to have a nightly food-party hits... say ... "That's Pigula Slop, and I NEVER eat Pigula Slop! even if it's just one bite".

Every single thought, physical sensation and emotion that even remotely suggest that you break your Food Plan and have an eating party at night originates from Pigula. When you hear Pigula Whisper, just look it square in the eyes and say "I will never eat your damn Slop again! Now go back to your coffin and shut up!"

If you're able to easily recognize and ignore the Whisper then do just that. But if that's not working for you, if the Whisper seems too compelling, then don't just think logically about your thought or emotion being a Pigula Whisper, aggressively order Pigula back to its coffin. Having that conversation can help you separate your higher self from Pigula and strengthens your control over your urges. It might sound a bit silly that we're telling you to have conversations with yourself. But it's vitally important that you do! *(And you only need to do it until you can reliably recognize and ignore any given Pigula Whisper.)*

One last tip: Have these conversations internally. If you walk around the house shouting at Pigula, there's a chance your family and/or your friends will commit you to a 72-hour psychiatric hold... and we don't want that!

Now Pigula will resist going back to its coffin. It will do everything in its power to make you break your commitment and eat. And that brings us to our next point...

You do not have to be comfortable to stick to your food plan – In fact, since most people have been partying with food at night for a few years *(or decades)* by the time they read this book, it's pretty much guaranteed that in the first few weeks while trying to break this habit, you'll feel uncomfortable – **probably very uncomfortable!**

However, if you eat adequately, and thoroughly nourish yourself throughout the day then it's perfectly ok for you to feel uncomfortable at night *(at first)*. In fact, it's more than OK, it means Pigula is suffering! You are breaking its hold on your mind and body—this is a painful process. And because you and Pigula are still entwined, you'll feel the pain as well. Provided you haven't created a significant nutritional or caloric deficiency this is a GOOD pain!

If you keep resisting, the urge and uncomfortable feelings *(both mental and physical)* will dissipate until they are no longer there. But this won't happen if you do either of the following things:

1. Give in to Pigula and eat outside of your food plan *(we'll show you how to create one just a few chapters from now)*. See, each time you DO give-in to Pigula you'll reinforce the nighttime eating habit and restore Pigula's power. Now, having said that, mistakes happen, and we'll teach you how to recover from them. For now, please go into this process with a 100% commitment to break Pigula's power over you by NEVER giving in to its alluring whispers, no matter how uncomfortable/hungry/angry/sad

you may become.

2. If you do not eat adequately throughout the day. This is Pigula's #1 secret tool. It convinces you you're "not really hungry" during the day, that "you're not a morning food person" and that "you can lose a lot of weight fast if you eat very little during the day." It will also attempt to convince you that because you can now use the tools we'll give you in this book to lock Pigula away, you'll be able to "lose a ton of weight" and should accelerate this by undereating during the day.

BIG mistake! Listening to these Whispers sets you up to fail because if you don't adequately eat during the day, you'll feel starving by nighttime. And then, much the same way you can NOT train yourself to never pee, you won't be able to resist the hunger. This can lead to massive binging in the evening which will restores all of Pigula's power *(and then some!)*

To sum up... the key is making a 100% commitment to withstand any nasty physical feeling, thought or sensation in order to avoid eating off your Food Plan in the evening!

Remember: The level of discomfort, as well as the nastiness of Pigula's command will decrease quickly, but you MUST go through the initial battle with Pigula in order to win.

Lastly, you'll have to say goodbye to late-night food parties and the food high that comes with them. You'll also need to find another activity that brings you joy.

When you avoid partying with food at night you will NOT die.

But you won't get a Food High either.

You'll just kill the craving and go on with your evening.

This will NOT be exhilarating.

You will experience a sense of contentment and increased confidence, but these are very balanced, low-key feelings. They do not resemble the thrill of the sugar-rush that comes along with the nighttime eating-party.

There's a reason why throughout this book we referred to the action of overeating at night as "Partying with Food." See, the act of overeating at night is unfortunately also a great source of short-term fun and pleasure.

And if you've been doing it for a while then you've become accustomed to have your own little party at night *(which usually includes a bit of a sugar-high).* That's a hard thing to give up.

This is why Pigula's whisper "But our life will be nothing but boredom and pain without nighttime eating" is so compelling. It actually has a point. But please consider the following...

Once you stop overeating at night and getting high with food, you CAN replace the source of exhilaration in your life. For us *(Yoav and I),* writing has become a source of pleasure. We love writing and find it exhilarating. We no longer need the sugar for exhilaration. For other people it's hugging their kids, playing with their dogs, walking in nature, doing art, music, engaging in more projects around the house or at work... something!

You might need to explore a few activities before you home in on *your* alternative source of exhilaration, but we promise you it's there. It might be something you loved doing as a child *(even if you weren't good at it).* Drawing or playing an instrument can be tremendously rewarding even if you'll never win an award for doing that. My partner Yoav draws like an untalented 5-year old but tells me drawing just makes him happy and he figured out that he doesn't need anyone's approval to be happy... so he just draws!

Last, please remember nighttime food parties come with a *horrific* price. Your health and your self-esteem are just a few things damaged with each indulgence.

Whenever Pigula Whispers to you that life is too sad without the nighttime food parties, consider what You sacrifice when you DO engage in them!

Is it worth it?

We think not!

CHAPTER 4: HOW MUCH TIME AND WILLPOWER IS REQUIRED TO CAGE PIGULA FOR GOOD?

The more times you compel Pigula back to its coffin the weaker it will get (it won't feed and get weaker by the day)!

Think of it this way...

When you tie your shoes, are you 100% concentrated on the task? Do you use all your consciousness to make the loops and tie the knot? Or do perform this task automatically while thinking of a million other things?

If you are like 99.9% of people, you need to allocate very little conscious effort to tying your shoes. You've trained your mind to perform the task and now there's a little part of *it (let's call it the shoe-tying pixie)* that automatically ties your shoes.

But the 'shoe tying pixie' part of your brain doesn't try to CONTROL YOU.

This is because your brain isn't rewarded if you tie your shoes repeatedly.

Pigula ,however, is an extremely powerful part of your mind because each time you overate at night, you strengthened the habit of nighttime eating with a very potent reward, made out of sugar and fat, and all the tasty things our body craves at the most primitive level.

So Pigula, like the shoe-tying pixie, is a semi-automatic process in your mind that compels you to eat at night.

But unlike the shoe-tying pixie, it is VERY POWERFUL!

This monster, however, has a huge weakness. Because it is a behavioral *pattern (it was created and strengthened by repeated rewards),* you can easily weaken it by depriving it of its reward.

And its power wll decline rapidly!

The first time might take a tremendous amount of effort.

The second, third and fourth time might be almost as difficult.

By the fifth time it'll be noticeably easier

In 10 days, it'll be substantially weaker.

And in 30-60 days it'll be a shadow of itself.

At this point some of our clients think they've beat Pigula for good and even though they can skip the nightly food-party as easily as they can have them... they decide to indulge because ... "they've mastered Pigula"

They're wrong!

You can never totally obliterate Pigula ... the nighttime overeating habit is only dormant... buried under a new set of habits... but if you let Pigula out for a few nights and let it once again compel you to overeat, it will grow as strong as it was before... The physical urge will return and now Pigula will be armed with the argument that no matter how hard you try it will always come back to life.

What you can do ... is lock Pigula in its cage forever, as long as you don't willfully let it out!!!

Therefore, once you have Pigula secured in its coffin, you must remain vigilant and not entertain it's Whispers even if they can barely be heard.

Reducing the amount of willpower required to fight Pigula by 90%

Imagine you had a tool that would allow you to catch Pigula immediately whenever it tried to compel you to eat.

A tool that would allow you to win every argument with it with ease.

A tool that would reduce the bartering, begging, whispering and whining around food at night by 90%.

A tool that would reduce all decision making around food by 90%.

Well... such a tool exists.

It's called "Food Rules".

And we've used food rules with tens of thousands of "Never Binge Again" readers and clients to reduce the amount of willpower it takes to control their binge eating dramatically.

In the next chapter we'll discuss the general food rules as they were introduced in Never Binge Again, this is extremely useful because rules can help you to change any eating behavior... not just nighttime overeating.

But in the following chapters, we will discuss how to create specific food rules to deal with night-time eating.

Rules so effective that Pigula will turn into a bat and flee if you just put them down on paper!

Here's how it's done...

CHAPTER 5: HOW TO HEAR PIGULA'S WHISPERS EVERY SINGLE TIME

To truly dominate Pigula we need to distinguish its Whispers from our own rational hunger. You'll need to make a concrete Food Plan with your own specific Food Rules *(even JUST ONE rule to get started)... and then definitively commit.*

Pigula hates rules and will do its very best to destroy the integrity of any you may set. This is why you must take 100% ownership and responsibility. It's also why every rule—*and your Food Plan as a whole*—must be set with 100% clarity. Otherwise, Pigula can use "fuzzy lines" and "diets you're just trying out for a while" to mercilessly assail your integrity and confidence.

You simply must...

Create your own Food Plan

You'll need to thoroughly embrace your own Food Plan, comprised solely of your own Food Rules. Why yours and not some diet guru's, nutritionist's, and/or weight loss doctor's? Because after you're five years old nobody can follow you around making sure you eat right, that's why.

Of course, you can and should get expert advice.

By all means, read health books, and work with experts you trust to inform your thinking. But if you're reading *this* book, odds are you've already done so. In fact, we'd be willing to bet Yoav's left kidney—*and he's rather fond of that one*—you've got a pretty good idea of what a well-balanced, nourishing, and reasonable diet looks like.

It'd work too, if you'd only stick to it!

So, let's skip all the "Mama said eat your vegetables" stuff and cut right to the "stick to it" part...

If you're finally going to stick to a plan, you'll need to OWN it — 100%.

After all, whose hands are going to grab the car keys, start the engine, drive to the market, put the food in the cart, take out the money, give it to the cashier, put the bags in the trunk, bring them inside, put them away, choose the meals, prepare them, get out the fork, stick it in, pick it up to your lips and put it in your mouth?

Yours.

Not your doctor's, nutritionist's, diet guru's, or therapist's hands, that's for sure! And it's a good thing, too, because for all their well-meaning advice and expertise, none of these people could follow you around 24 hours a day, even if they wanted to do so.

The ONLY way you're ever going to succeed is if you accept 100% responsibility for every bite and swallow. You see, "trying out" professional diet plans is a type of dependency which sets Pigula up to retake control like this:

> "Must've been a bad diet plan that nutritionist, doctor, or diet-guru recommended. You'll have to talk to them about it. Or maybe we need to find someone else to follow. Oh well, in the meantime we might as well just Party. Yummy!!!" — Sincerely, Pigula

So, this one's up to you. You're completely and utterly responsible — 100%, not 99.999%. ONE HUNDRED PERCENT. Get it?

Breathe for a moment here and listen for your Pig's inevitable Squeal:

> "Wait just a minute here! This book itself is a diet book too, isn't it? After all Glenn and Yoav are just two guys trying to make a buck with weight-loss advice. So, go ahead, try it out for a while. Sooner or later you'll cheat like you always do, and then I'll be free to Party with me at night again. In fact, why wait? Let's do it NOW! Yippee!!!" – Sincerely, Pigula

What a greedy vampire. Lock him in his coffin!

How to own your Food Plan 100%

This might seem obvious but...

The best way to own your Food Plan is to write it down.

Every single Food rule... and the Plan as a whole.

100%, unambiguously.

That means, if 10 people were to review your plan and watch how you ate all day long, they'd *unanimously* agree whether you were on it or off it. Not 9 of them. ALL of them.

However, your Food Plan is a very private matter. So, this

"would 10 people agree" test is only a thought experiment to help YOU judge whether you've articulated it clearly and precisely.

The reason you want to spell out your plan with enough precision that 10 people could agree is because ambiguity is Pigula's best friend...

Ambiguity is a yellow light, not a red one...

And Pigula will go 100 miles per hour from a quarter mile away to speed through a yellow light. You can count on it, every time.

When the specifics are laid out in incontrovertible detail, however, you convert fuzzy yellow lights into red, and it becomes impossible for Pigula to run the light without getting caught—because you'll immediately recognize any thought suggesting you run the light as Pigula's Whisper ...

...which you can promptly ignore — not argue or debate with, not console, not attend to in any way...

Ignore.

There's NO use trying to reason with Pigula. It doesn't care for your well-being. All it wants is to Party with food, and it will twist around every last bit of information and attention you provide in order to persuade you to feed it. Therefore, we starve Pigula of information and attention at every turn.

If you simply ignore Pigula, the red lights will hold forever.

Why?

Because YOU are the only one who can put your foot on the gas and run the lights — *no matter how much Pigula may protest or try to convince you otherwise.*

The only danger is in not recognizing Pigula's Whisper for what it is. *The only danger is thinking Pigula is you.* That's why we're such sticklers for a precisely defined plan.

You do NOT have to follow anyone else's guidelines for writing up your Food Plan. Do it in whatever manner suits you best.

After all, it's your Plan. And as long as it's 100% unambiguous, clear, and nutritionally sound, it will suffice.

In a moment, we'll provide a simple set of guidelines for constructing your Food Plan. However, we must first warn you, Pigula will scream in response to this part of the book than any other. Just continue to ignore its objections and remember four important things:

> ➢ (1) Even though we'll be talking about how to use "Never" and "Always" kinds of rules to provide clarity, these are NOT required elements of this program—*you can construct healthy and effective Food Plans entirely without them. (Download the free food plan starter templates from www.NeverBingeAgain.com for examples)...*
>
> ➢ (2) The goal is to create the *LEAST* severe Food Plan which still protects you. Only you can know how to comprise this. But the purpose of the plan is to give you an unshakable sense of confidence, not turn you into a "Food Nazi" ...
>
> ➢ (3) Even though we'll push any semblance of a doubt in our ability to keep to your Food Plan out of our minds so we can "pedal up the hill" with 100% confidence, we do have a plan for gently forgiving ourselves and quickly resuming course if mistakes are made.
>
> ➢ (4) You don't have to create the whole Food Plan

at once. In fact, most people do better by creating just ONE Food Rule (we'll recommend the one we find the most helpful to deal with nighttime overeating in the next chapter) ... with NO concern about losing weight. Only then—*after adhering to the rule successfully for a few weeks to a few months and reclaiming their sense of hope, enthusiasm, and power*—do they venture forth into a full Food Plan with a multitude of rules. *(And, generally speaking, only then do they also begin to adjust these rules to include weight loss as a goal. Stop partying at night and gaining weight first. Get control. Reclaim your power. Lose weight later.)*

With this framework in mind, let's talk about:

A Simple Set of Guidelines for Constructing a Food Plan

As long as your Food Plan is easy to remember, unambiguous, and nutritionally complete you can make it work. Here are some simple categories of Food Rules you may wish to consider:

➢ **NEVERS:** What foods, drinks, and behaviors will you *never* indulge in again as long as you live?

➢ **ALWAYS:** What will you *always* do regarding food, drink, and food behaviors? *(For example, "I always eat six servings of fruit and vegetables each calendar day" or "I always write down what I may potentially eat the next day before I go to bed to force myself to think through any difficult spots.")*

➢ **UNRESTRICTED:** What foods, drinks, and food behaviors will you permit yourself to have *without restriction?*

➢ **CONDITIONALS:** What foods, drinks, and behaviors will you permit only at certain times, in certain amounts, and/or restricted by other *conditions? (Specify these in exquisite detail so there's no ambiguity about when the light is red vs. green. Avoid yellow lights because in Pigula's way of thinking, yellow = bright green.)*

There are a few different variables involved in constructing a Food Plan, so it's somewhat more difficult to quit overeating at night than to stop abusing drugs, cigarettes, or alcohol. With the latter you can just quit. But with food, you can't just quit eating.

Pigula will try to defeat you with this fact. A good Food Plan eliminates the possibility.

Once you're armed with a crystal-clear plan, you'll quickly catch on to Pigula's handful of sneaky strategies, no matter how long you've previously been fooled. Therefore, we're going to spend considerable time illustrating how to adopt Nevers, Always, Unrestricted, and Conditionals, and make them stick, specifically for nighttime overeaters!

Let's start with NEVER.

Never is the simplest and clearest red light of all. Creating even one Never is a great way to learn how to hear Pigula's Squeals because it clearly draws the line between your food vs. Pigula Slop. Setting even one Never is how you begin your new life.

> "OK, OK. If you're going to insist on doing something to slow down for a while, how about we just eat a salad tonight? I could definitely live with *that*. But whatever
> you do just don't say NEVER!" - Sincerely, Pigula

How to Never Do Something (Anything) Again

NEVER is a word you won't hear much in our culture when it comes to food, alcohol, drugs, or any other pleasurable substance. That's a shame, because it's one of the most powerful words for taking permanent control over Pigula.

If you can't say you'll NEVER do *something* again *(or never engage in a particular food behavior again)*, Pigula knows it's only a matter of time until it gains the upper hand. If we define a "overeating" as engaging in any eating behavior which contradicts your Food Plan, then at very minimum we must be able to say we will NEVER overeat again.

So, we will carefully define a livable and acceptable Food Plan and then NEVER break it again!

If you think about it, it's very odd how unwilling we've become to say NEVER when it comes to things which have caused so much misery in our lives. There are many behaviors we expect people never to engage in. So why not add one more when you have so much to gain?

➢ We expect responsible members of society to NEVER kill, rape, or steal...

➢ We expect people with life threatening allergies to avoid certain substances for the rest of their lives *(for example, there are some people who simply can't eat peanuts... EVER)*...

➢ We expect people to NEVER act on their sexual impulses in public...

➢ And married persons are supposed to confine their romantic and sexual adventures to each other. We even have a legal contract — *the marriage license* — which formalizes this understanding.

In fact, we've all learned to NEVER do many things just to get through everyday life:

- Never put your hand on a hot stove or in the electric socket
- Never threaten a political official with bodily harm
- Never grab a knife on the sharp end

And some of our 'Nevers' are so strongly ingrained we don't even realize they're learned behaviors. For example:

- Never pass gas at the table when dining with others
- Never grab a total stranger and kiss them on the lips
- Never sit at the teacher's desk in school
- Never take off your shoes and socks in church
- Never kick a policeman in the tushy

By the time most children are 10 years old they've naturally learned all of these things — and if they can do it, so can you. Adding one more 'Never' is child's play, no matter how much short-term pleasure one must sacrifice, and no matter what your Pig says!

> *"Are you really going to let these guy tell us to NEVER eat something again? C'mon, have a spine!!"*
> *– Sincerely, Your "Starving" Pigula*

IMPORTANT: Despite what Pigula may say, nobody is telling you what to do. In fact, that's the whole point.

Until now you've allowed Pigula to impose its will as if you were its slave. The information in this section gives YOU the power to make *permanent* decisions without Pigula's pernicious influence. The moment you put even one Never in your Food Rules, you've begun to Lock Pigula in its coffin!

Always

Always is Never's best friend. Defining some things you will ALWAYS do — and acting on these *commitments* — will give you even more confidence in your ability to cage the Pig.

Yes ALWAYS — you know, as in every day for the rest of your life.

Your 'Always' list should include general self-care in addition to food specific behaviors. For example, maybe you always start the day with a glass of water. Or maybe you always shower in the evening to help you get to sleep without extra food. Maybe you always meditate, exercise, or make fresh vegetable juice.

Maybe you always eat an apple before lunch...

Or maybe you don't *always* do anything.

Whatever you put here, just remember "always" and "never" are sacred vows. They become something the Pig can't assail, no matter how hard it tries, because the motives behind any Squeal suggesting an exception will be recognized immediately.

But as soon as you declare an intention which interferes with Pigula's yummy nighttime parties, it will begin trying hard to defeat you. That's its job. You see, Pigula genuinely believes it will die without its precious slop. But you will prevail as long as you remember Pigula's Whispers are not your own thinking.

For example, suppose you always drink a soothing cup of decaffeinated tea an hour after your last meal. Always! As soon as you declare this rule, Pigula may say something like:

> "You can't say ALWAYS! How could you ever know that? One evening you'll be busy and forget. Or maybe you just won't feel like it. Some you simply won't have the time.

> Then you'll have broken your silly vow. These ridiculous rules obviously don't matter since you can't possibly stick with them. We might as well just go PARTYYYYY!" —Sincerely, Pigula

To prevail, you need only dismiss this as a "Whisper".

Don't argue with Pigula.

You don't need to, because Pigula is powerless to do anything without your consent. If Pigula could act on its own behalf it would immediately do so without asking. The very fact it talks *at all* proves its only hope is to convince you with its lies.

All that's necessary is to ignore it.

Notwithstanding this, let's dispute its points one by one, just to show you how ridiculous Pigula's arguments can be:

"You can't possibly mean 'Always'. Nobody can ever know what they're always going to do!"

This is Pigula's first attempt to pull the wool over your eyes. It says "You can't always do *anything!*" What a negative, confidence-destroying message.

Would you ever tell a young child: "Listen little Bobby, there's NO hope of remembering to brush your teeth, tie your shoes, and get dressed all by yourself every day. Just get that idea out of your head. You might as well just give up and accept you'll be a dependent little child the rest of your life... no matter what the big boys do."

Of course you wouldn't! Then why let Pigula talk to you that way?

The truth is there are many, many things people ALWAYS do

daily...

- They turn off their alarm
- Roll out of bed
- Pee in the toilet
- Brush their teeth
- Etc.
- You can add one more ALWAYS anytime you want!

Let's go on...

> "One evening you'll forget.
> And then you'll have broken your silly vow."

Pigula wants you to *plan to forget* your vow. But the very nature of a vow is a *plan to remember*. Which is more constructive? Which is more likely to improve your life?

The answer is obvious. So why would anyone ever make a plan to forget when we, as human beings, have the ability to plan to remember? People don't do that. Pigula(s) do!

Any doubt you have about your ability to ALWAYS do something is 100% driven by Pigula's desire to have you break your vow. It doesn't care what impact this has on your confidence, self-esteem, health, or loved ones. Pigula is an anarchist and will try to destroy any structure which interferes with its nightly food orgies — at the expense of all your goals and aspirations. It has only contempt for your higher plans. Which is why we owe it nothing but contempt in return.

The truth is there are many things we're perfectly capable of remembering to do every single day. For example, taking care of our children.

> "Sorry little Sarah, I'm afraid I won't be giving you anything to eat or drink today. And you'll just have to stay up all night because Daddy can't possibly remember to put you to bed either" — How Pigula would take care of a small child

We also drive our cars home every day and park them in a safe spot – *instead of the lawn or the neighbor's rose garden* – even though the latter might be more convenient. We eat and/or drink enough to sustain us through one more day. And we put ourselves to bed every night somewhere at least reasonably safe and comfortable *(as opposed to lying down outside in our front yards without a tent or sleeping bag)*

> "These rules are just silly… obviously they don't matter at all since you can't possibly stick with them."

See how Pigula attempts to undermine even your simplest effort at positive, healthy change? It doesn't care if you die of dehydration. It must subvert your confidence and impulse control or else it won't get any more Slop *(ever)*. Knowing this, it's clear we can't ever take it seriously.

> "You might as well just let me PARTY!"

Pigula's true nature comes out at last. The Binge is all it was after all along.

But just for argument's sake, suppose you DID break your plan to always drink a soothing cup of decaffeinated tea every evening. Does it naturally follow you should go out and buy several bags of Doritos, a box of donuts, a pound of chocolate bars… and go to town on them all at once?

Of course not. If you forget to brush your teeth one morning, are you obligated to pick up a hammer and bang them all out? It's ridiculous.

Pidula's Whispers may *seem* rational on their surface, but they never are. *(Never—as in never, ever, ever, ever, ever, EVER!)*

Pigula can appear very appealing *at first* because of its ability to leverage a vulnerability in your survival drive. But when you hold its Whisper up to the light of day it NEVER makes any sense.

Just ignore Pigula's Whisper when you hear it. Period, end of story.

UNRESTRICTED

Some people find it helpful to list out those things they can eat and/or drink in unlimited quantities without concern. Others just designate the 'Unrestricted' category as being everything that is not specifically listed on their restricted list.

Usually the 'Unrestricted' category is comprised of healthy "go to" foods you feel good about eating. For example, perhaps you want to allow as many leafy greens, cruciferous vegetables, green tea, beans, berries, clean water, etc., as you desire.

Or maybe you feel safer with NEVER and CONDITIONAL rules for everything... and prefer not to leave anything unrestricted. It's completely up to you!

However you handle your 'Unconditional' section, just be sure you remember Pigula's favorite con:

> "We simply MUST cheat this one time only or else we'll never be happy again!"

— Sincerely, Pigula

Regardless of how you construct your 'Unrestricted' category you must always ensure there is enough leeway in your overall Food Plan so you'll have enough to eat. Otherwise Pigula's Squeals start to sound more alluring — and you must always be able to dismiss them outright.

Humans evolved during times of intermittent famine. Our bodies are set up to go for long periods without eating. It takes a minimum of several weeks without food for most people to starve to death. What are the odds you're going to die (or become morbidly sad) if you go 12 hours without a meal? Slim to none!

There's NEVER a good reason to have a nighttime food orgy.

Pigula is NOT trying to take care of you by suggesting you'll be permanently unhappy if you don't make an exception to your Food Plan. Its purpose is NOT to make you happy or nourish your body but to destroy your Plan so it can go on an all-out Food Orgy.

Lock Pigula in its coffin and keep it there!

CONDITIONALS

Note: Conditional rules might not be the first choice for dealing with nighttime overeating, but they can prove to be very effective in creating an overall food plan. It is well worth your time to read this section.

There are some foods and drinks that might work for you only in certain situations, at certain times, or when accompanying certain behaviors.

Maybe you only allow yourself sports drinks after a certain

amount of exercise on a given calendar day.

Maybe you get to have a certain treasured meal only when dining out with friends, but no more than twice a week.

Maybe it's that you only eat chocolate on Saturday nights after dinner.

Or maybe you just eat pretzels on days when you take your son or daughter to a major league baseball game.

The point of the 'Conditional' category is to acknowledge certain foods, drinks, and food behaviors are only troublesome when left unregulated — *or only in certain situations.*

The limit on the conditions you impose only stems from your own imagination and experience. We're not necessarily suggesting any of the examples above are good or bad. But we will leave you with one caution: Avoid letting your 'Conditional' section become *too* complex. It's very difficult to remember complex rules when you're hungry, so the simpler the better.

Keep going over your conditions until they're expressed in the simplest possible language.

Fewer, clearer rules tend to work best.

For some people this is just a sentence or two, for others it's a whole page. Still others will have NO food or drink as 'Conditional' whatsoever.

The point is to go through the exercise and think through which foods, drinks, and food behaviors you don't need to give up entirely (specifically at night), but which still require *some* degree of control. It can also help articulate in writing your rationale for each of these conditions to ensure Pigula is not sneaking in some Whisper.

Last, if you find you're repeatedly struggling to find the right condition for a particular food, drink, or behavior, the odds are you'd do better to move it to the 'Never' section. *(This paragraph can save you years of painful struggle so you might want to re-read it)*

There you have it.

Never, Always, Unrestricted, and Conditional.

Four beautifully simple categories to create your own personal, self-contained legal system for governing your eating from here on.

Lastly, Pigula absolutely hates the idea of a crystal-clear Food Plan. It wants you to believe such a Plan will restrict your freedom. *But exactly the opposite is true.* Just as most great jazz players practice their scales for years before they can freely express their creative genius, so too will you need structure around food to truly enjoy not only your food, but ALL the freedom life has to offer:

THE QUESTION IS, WHO WILL BE FREE, YOU OR PIGULA?

The question isn't whether you'll have freedom of choice vs becoming enslaved to a Food Plan. The question is, will you choose to live your life as a slave to Pigula's impulses and demands, or put the beast in its coffin so you can exercise your freedom?

Besides, you already have a Food Plan whether you write it down or not! It's impossible to function each day without making decisions about what you'll never, always, sometimes, and conditionally eat. The problem is, most people make these decisions *unconsciously*.

For example, everyone *always* stops overeating at a certain point, even if that point is unhealthy. They might eat a whole pizza, but not five. And they certainly don't eat the box the pizza came in.

Almost everyone also *always* has their favorite treats too, consumed in just the right combinations and amounts.

And there are at least some things most people avoid entirely for reasons of taste, convenience, or health.

Since you already DO have a Food Plan, I'm only suggesting you take control. Make it conscious and evaluate it with the full force of your intellect. Write the darn thing down!

WARNING – DON'T CREATE AN OVERLY RESTRICTIVE FOOD PLAN

Some people confuse our emphasis on clarity, focus, and written, unbreakable Food Rules with the kind of restriction which can stimulate bulimia and/or anorexia. This is not our intention at all.

There are two ways in which restrictive eating may lead to problem, and it's important you consider them both before creating your Food Plan...

The first is restricting the number of calories you consume to such a degree you become constantly hungry. When you're constantly hungry, Pigula's Whispers become more and more powerful and many people eventually break down and Binge. That's why we STRONGLY ADVISE AGAINST severely restricting your calorie intake. It's better to first create rules that are easy to follow. This allows you to eliminate the overeating behavior. Then, once you're confident in your ability to control Pigula, you can "go on a diet" and eliminate some of your caloric intake – but again – the best way to do this is in moderation.

The second way restrictive eating can be harmful is if you have previously been diagnosed with an eating disorder such as anorexia or bulimia, and/or if you've used restrictive eating in the past as a tool to avoid eating altogether and/or to avoid eating nutritionally important types of foods.

If you've been diagnosed with an eating disorder and/or have used restrictive eating before to drastically reduce your caloric intake beyond safe levels, then you should be very careful about creating eating rules. It does not mean that you can't use this method, because after all, everyone needs a Food Plan. However, in this case we advise you only create rules with the help of a psychologist/psychiatrist and a dietician so you do not fall into the trap of abusing the food rules as you've done in the past.

However, if you are confident in your ability to create a healthy Food Plan which provides your body enough calories and nutrition—*and your only real concern is your ability to stick to it*—then by all means, please proceed!

Now, we've purposefully avoided recommending any particular Food Plan and/or positioning ourselves as a dietary or nutritional experts because the moment we even hint at telling you what to eat, Pigula will inevitably Squeal "We could NEVER eat like that! You might as well stop right here"

See, Pigula would LOVE to turn this into a big nutritional debate because there's still a lot of controversy about what constitutes the ideal diet. And Pigula knows that immersing you in this controversy would distract you from the main point, which is permanently committing to a Food Plan of *your own* design, using *your own* best thinking.

But now you're aware of its diabolical strategy, so you won't be vulnerable to it...

FREE STARTER TEMPLATES FOR YOUR PERSONAL FOOD PLAN

Find a great starting point no matter what you personally believe is the healthiest way to eat! The templates are part of the FREE book bonuses available on the website. When you download them you'll also find a Custom Food Plan Worksheet to take you through the creation of your own plan in much more detail.

Click Here Now to Download:
www.NeverBingeAgain.com

Are you ready to create your first (and most important) food rule?

A food rule that scares Pigula more than the light of day?

Yes?

Good!

Read on...

CHAPTER 6: SUNDOWN DEMARCATION RULES ARE THE MOST IMPORTANT RULES YOU'LL EVER CREATE!

Day One – The Sundown Demarcation Line

In virtually every vampire movie there's a very clear distinction between daylight and dark. The tension is palpable after the sun goes down. The audience knows when they're watching the part of the movie where the characters are safe, and the part where they are in serious peril from the creature. The music changes. The lighting is much different. The heroes adopt a very different mindset and allocate their mental and physical energies *much* differently before vs. after dark.

So too do clients and readers who've successfully overcome nighttime overeating know when Pigula is out for the hunt vs. sleeping it off in his coffin. They have clear cut-off times which indicate when eating for the day is over...

After all, if you don't know when nighttime is, how can you possibly discern what it means to overeat at night? The actual demarcation hour varies greatly from client to client, however, and does not necessarily correspond with when the sun goes down in the real world. There are some clients who live in the far north where sundown swings wildly – it could be as late as 11 pm in the summer and as early as 2 pm in the winter. Literally using darkness to signal the end of the day's eating isn't practical in certain latitudes of the modern world.

Therefore, successful clients tend to have picked a time on the clock. For example, "I will never eat after 8 pm again." The actual hour varies greatly too, mostly to accommodate work and/or parenting schedules. What's important is that there is a very definite and specific known cut-off time. Finally, many people specify an exception if they are out to dinner with others and/or at some sort of social and/or work function which involves a meal. This doesn't seem to interfere with their success.

Not surprisingly, many clients *also* found it necessary to know when the sun came UP—when food would once again be permitted. "I will never again consume calories between 9 pm and 5 am", for example. *(Also with exceptions for socializing and/or food related work functions, etc).*

Finally, not everyone engaged in a total fast during the "nighttime" hours. Some had rules which permitted low-calorie/low-digestive burden exceptions such as unsauced vegetables, coffee and/or tea with stevia, etc.

Knowing when the "sun goes down and comes up" is necessary for you to define what nighttime overeating means. Without this clear cut-off time you have no way of knowing whether you have successfully kept Pigula in its coffin.

Day One - Practical Steps

Step 1: Determine Your Sundown Demarcation Line

Take stock of when you think it would be best to initially set your personal sundown. Will it be at a specific hour? Related to a specific event, perhaps like finishing one plate of food at dinner? And determine when your personal sunrise is too! Write down your reasons in detail.

Step 2: Write Down Your Sundown Demarcation Line Rules

After determining your personal sundown and sunrise times and ensuring you've written down your reasons, write out a set of Never Binge Again rules (explained in chapter 5) that define your behavior around the demarcation line. Here are some examples for such rules (you can adopt them, customize them or create altogether different rules):

Example 1:

I will never consume calories after dinner and until breakfast

Dinner – The last meal of the day that occurs after I get home from work and before I settle down (watch TV, Read, etc.')

Breakfast – The first thing I eat after 6 am

Example 2:

I will never consume calories after 8 pm and before 6 am except when eating out

I will never consume calories at home after I eat out in the evening

Example 3:

I will never again consume calories after dinner *(whether I eat at home or out with friends.)*

Example 4:

At parties and/or when dining out with friends I will never again drink more than 2 alcoholic beverages after dinner

Except for the aforementioned drinks, I will never consume calories between dinner and breakfast.

Note: It is up to you to create the set of rules that will allow you the greatest degree of freedom while making sure that they do not contain loop holes that will allow Pigula to escape its coffin and convince you to binge! And since you've known Pigula for ages, you probably have a very good idea which rules you should put into place.

Step 3: Vow to Follow These Rules Forevermore

Now, take a breath, put your hand on your heart, and recite the following statement "I solemnly commit to forevermore follow my sundown demarcation rules!"

Please note we are using the word "forevermore" in a kind of funky way. This is because we are presenting these rules to Pigula as if it were set in stone, even though we know we can change the criteria with serious forethought and consideration later.

As we previously discussed, when you tell a two year old child (s)he can never cross the street without holding your hand, you're technically lying to him or her because you full well know you are going to teach them how to cross on their own in five or six years. But it's just too dangerous for that child to even THINK about crossing the street on their own at two years old.

So, we present the rule to them as if it were set in stone.

It's too dangerous to let Pigula think the rules are flexible too, so we also present your Food Rules to it as if they were set in stone. It's OK to lie to Pigula. After all, Pigula has been lying to you for years, hasn't it?

How to Harness the Immense Power of Sundown Demarcation Rules

Defining the sundown demarcation rules is the EXTREMELY IMPORTANT. These are the rules which allow you to immediately hear ALL OF PIGULAS WHISPERS because every thought which even remotely suggests you ever violate the Sundown Demarcation rules is by definition a Pigula Whisper. Once you understand this and can finally distinguish Pigula's thoughts from your own, you'll have the power force Pigula back to its coffin at will!

No matter what excuse, whine or whisper that vile creature presents you with simply tell it...

> "I see what you're trying to do here Pigula! I will not let you have a food orgy! Now shut up and go back to your coffin!"

That is why it is exceptionally important you define your own demarcation rules, write them down, and commit to them 100%!

Doing anything else is to leave the door wide open for Pigula.

At this point, Pigula will be screaming at the top of its lungs trying to persuade you to avoid writing down these rules...

> "These guys are two freaking nut jobs! Writing

> rules? Solemnly swearing? What are we, children? Tell them to F*#K OFF!!! We are not children!"

That's because it knows that when you define your demarcation line rules in writing and commit to them you will have the power to shut the door of its coffin every single night... so it is deathly afraid.

In fact, once Pigula understands you are serious about your plans to put your sundown demarcation rules in writing it will switch to flat-out begging and pleading!

> "Are we really going to stop partying with food at night? That's the ONE THING we really love. The one thing that gives us pleasure. Are we really going to live a miserable, anxious life with no reprieve from the stress and self-doubt? Don't do it to us! Pleeeaaaasssseeee!"

But you know better. You know these nightly binges can only MASK the anxiety, loneliness, and self-doubt for a few hours. You also know that in reality your nighttime overeating episodes are probably the biggest contributors to all of the self-doubt and inner stress you want to eliminate. You know these binges are damaging your health, destroying your self-esteem, and preventing you from feeling and looking great. *(Yes, you can feel and look great, don't let Pigula tell you otherwise!)*

But Pigula doesn't care about that. It doesn't want to help you in the slightest. Pigula only wants its food orgy. The hell with you and what you want, it says.

Well... that stops now!

Write your rules, commit to them 100%, and let's close the

door on this monster forever!

Days Two – How to Customize a Ritual and Decompression Routine to Emphasize Your Personal Demarcation Line

Overview

In the vampire movies, sundown rituals make the characters feel safer. They know it's time to be more alert and execute every last trick they have to protect themselves from being bitten. In real life, we create and customize a Demarcation Ritual to help with the feeling you can and will keep Pigula in its coffin. Your personal Demarcation Ritual will serve as a potent reminder that your personal Demarcation Line has been crossed.

The Decompression Routine is what you do AFTER your Demarcation Ritual to emphasize that it IS indeed safe to wind down, let go of the day, and eventually drift off to sleep without overeating.

There are a variety of psychological reasons why rituals can be effective at binding anxiety and enhancing the ability to function in the face of fear, but the strongest one in our experience is that the ritual delays impulse *(lower brain)* and engages the cognitive function *(upper brain).* Having a ritual to mark the transition from eating to not eating in the evening is kind of like flexing your neocortex at Pigula and saying "I'm SO much stronger than you!" Even if the rituals themselves are constructed on superstitious beliefs, the muscle is still exercised and strengthened. Then, once the muscle is strong enough, you can flex it WITHOUT the ritual if you so choose.

In other words, at first, you'll obtain added protection against nighttime overeating utilizing a number of personalized rituals, in much the same way the populace of yesteryear used rituals to make them feel safe from the vampires of lore. Some of you may choose to keep these rituals indefinitely as you'll discover a certain security and confidence within them. There's absolutely nothing wrong with that! It's completely unnecessary to abandon them once they are working.

But eventually, many of you will become so confident you've indeed gained total control over Pigula's previously effective hold on you, that you'll find the rituals unnecessary. You'll simply become a person who doesn't overeat at night. You'll always remember the time it seemed impossible to resist Pigula's commands, but in a way not dissimilar to how you used to be terrified of the boogeyman as a child in the dark. It'll become something you just grew out of, and you'll have confidence in your ability to permanently maintain your new habits and routines.

Successful Rituals Used by Our Clients and Readers

The actual rituals among successful clients and readers were varied, and a matter of personal preference, but followed a pattern with three clear elements: (1) Physical demarcation; (2) physical cleansing and; (3) transition to alternative activities, which may include "allowed" foods or snacks.

Physical demarcation mostly involved going to another room, ideally in another part of the house: "What works best for me is to go upstairs right after dinner. I live in a two-level home with the kitchen on first floor. I take everything I need for the night upstairs with me - water, a book, etc. And I don't come back down and/or go through kitchen again for night.

This was often accompanied by a mantra spoken out loud such as "kitchen's closed", as well as a physical act which accentuated the point, such as clapping one's hands three times as if one were dusting them off, or loudly opening and closing the kitchen cabinets in similar fashion.

Many clients paired their "separate part of the house after dinner" routine with a special rule which prevented them from eating while watching television and/or working on the computer. The mindless eating which occurs in front of a screen seemed to make them forget about the clearly demarcated food boundary ("when the sun sets"). Some went so far as to create a "I will only ever consume calories while sitting at a table again" rule.

Physical cleansing was largely focused on the mouth, with most clients indicating they brushed their teeth and/or used mouth wash after their last meal. But many successful people also took a shower and/or a bath whenever they felt tempted, and some said their cravings were diminished when they engaged in self-care *for the skin*. Moisturizing and exfoliating were chief amongst these routines.

A large proportion of people who stopped nighttime overeating would also allow themselves a low and/or no-calorie drink —often served warm. *More importantly, they would RELISH their time with the drink*. For example: "I can have water, seltzer or mint tea. That's it. I put the seltzer in a huge glass with lots of ice. Sipping on it throughout the evening gives me something to do and hold when I'm anxious, frustrated, and/or want to eat. Mint tea goes in a huge mug and I carry it around the house as it seems to soothe that need to put something in my mouth."

Some people allowed a warm glass of almond milk, regular milk, or a turmeric latte made with almond milk and stevia.

Some made a dessert shake with almond milk and frozen berries and sometimes cocoa with dates. Others used sugar-free Jello and/or some additional protein before bed if they really had to eat something...

Generally speaking, however, we can't recommend eating after "sundown" because it's not really part of the majority success pattern we observed, and you're still reinforcing the pathways which say that eating is possible after the demarcation point *(It's better to add more to your dinner meal, for example, if you find you're legitimately still hungry before bed.)*

Other alternative activities in which people who'd stopped overeating at night engaged in included mostly knitting, crochet, crossword puzzles, jigsaw puzzles, and tracking both their food and night-fasting time. *(Some had a fasting app which allowed them to do this. The "Zero" app is a decent option.)*

Still other successful readers reported listening to educational audios. Many listened to our demonstration coaching sessions from the podcast for inspiration and motivation at this time. https://www.neverbingeagain.com/TheBlog/recorded-sessions/all-my-audios-all-in-one-place-updated/

What everyone who engaged in alternative activities had in common was a LOVE of that activity. They relished the time to engage in it just like the woman in the example above relished her mint tea and/or seltzer.

Nighttime eating appears to be partially driven by the need to decompress from the day, so successful clients and readers planned activities which helped them wind down and have a good night's sleep. Mostly the types of things you'd expect: Playing with animals, reading a good book, doing some journaling, meditation, taking a hot bath with Epsom Salt, aromatherapy, warm neck pillows, watching a good movie, talking through the day with a trusted loved one or friend, etc.

Many successful former nighttime overeaters also laid out their workout clothes and buzzed through a hypothetical food plan for the next day *(not for 100% compliance but just to spot any potentially difficult situations or scheduling conflicts which would make it hard to eat well)*...and wrote down at least three good things from the day for which they felt grateful or proud.

Just like demarcation rituals, the key to effective decompression time is customizing it for your own unique needs. Winding down before bed in just the way you want to is a critical part of overcoming nighttime eating. You need to put yourself in the right frame of mind to rest and restore throughout the night.

It's worth noting that establishing and maintaining a demarcation ritual and decompression routine is the weapon which seems to require some effort and experimentation... but it's worth it! As one reader said: *"This is far from effortless, but every night gets easier and easier, and the confidence which comes with that is priceless."*

Day Two - Practical Steps

Step 1: Decide on your own Demarcation Rituals and Decompression Routine

Review the three types of successful Demarcation Rituals and Decompression Routines in detail and ask yourself which seem most appealing to you. Which ones make you think "Yeah, I could do something like that!" Remember, these include:

- **Physical Demarcation:** For example, going to another room of the house with everything you need for the night. Clapping your hands three times as if you're loudly dusting them off and saying "kitchen's closed." What can you do and/or say to make it abundantly clear that nighttime has arrived, and everything is now *very* different regarding food until breakfast tomorrow?

➢ **Physical Cleansing**: For example, brushing your teeth and/or using mouthwash once dinner is done. Taking a shower or a bath. Cleansing, moisturizing, exfoliating, and/or other skin care routines. What might you like to do for your physical body?

➢ **A Transition to Alternative Activities**: What activities will be allowed and emphasized as you unwind and begin to let go of the day so you can be ready for sleep later on? What calories will be allowed? This may include some type of no and/or low-calorie drink like water, seltzer, mint tea, or warm almond milk with stevia, etc. Activities might include things like playing with animals, reading a good book, doing some journaling, meditation, taking a hot bath with Epsom Salt, aromatherapy, warm neck pillows, watching a good movie, talking through the day with a trusted loved one or friend, knitting, crossword puzzles, playing with the kids, journaling, etc. You might also consider setting things up for morning. What clothes will you wear? What else will you need ready and waiting for you?

Step 2: Add Rules to Your Food Plan

Put your Demarcation Ritual and Decompression Routine in writing. Be as detailed and specific as you can. What will you do or say? What's allowed vs. not allowed?

Now add to rules to your Food Plan to reflect this! Write it down and commit. Do it tonight!

Here are a few examples of rules you might add:

- I will always clap my hands three times as if I'm dusting them off and say "Kitchen's closed!" after I'm done eating the last meal of the day.

- I will always brush my teeth immediately after I finish dinner.

- I will always make myself a large cup of green tea and knit for at least 15 minutes immediately after dinner.

- I will eat only foods from my Unlimited Foods category after dinner.

- I will never eat in front of the TV again.

- I will never bring food into the living room while I'm at home by myself.

- I will only ever eat sitting down at a table with a table, fork and knife.

You get the point.

To avoid feeling overwhelmed, when starting out your nightly routine, make sure you begin with one or two simple rules. Once implementing those rules becomes routine, you can add more to protect you if you feel they are necessary.

Day Three – Mantras

Please don't let the brevity of this section detract from its importance. See, most people who've successfully overcome nighttime overeating have developed a catch phrase or mantra which they repeat to help neutralize Pigula's post-demarcation cravings. These mantras are easy to list, but each is extremely powerful in its own right. Some of them have become popular on our free readers forum on Facebook (www.NeverBingeAgainForum.com) Several clients use more than one. Here are examples:

- **"Dinner and Done!"** This has become a popular mantra on our forum begun by an enthusiastic woman named Liv R. who you can hear in several of the podcasts. It reflects the extremely slippery slide of even *thinking* of eating anything after the evening meal. Liv recently posted that she genuinely believes she's not only become a person who doesn't binge eat at night, she's become someone who just doesn't binge eat, period.

- **"Don't start!"** Virtually everyone who stopped overeating at night was painfully aware that Pigula's "just one little bite before bedtime" Whisper was a deadly lie. "Don't start" encapsulates the notion that one bite can be a tragedy. One woman paired this with her goal weight to trigger her WHY. For example, "Don't start – 135!" *(If 135 pounds were your goal weight. The woman who first mentioned this mantra actually was from overseas, so her mantra was in kilos.)*

- **"I Can Have It in the Morning If I Really Want It!"** This type of mantra is largely used to manage nighttime cravings for foods which were otherwise *on-plan*, just not appropriate "after the sun sets." A corresponding mantra to help manage *off-plan* cravings is "I can have it tomorrow if I really want it." You can change your Food Plan whenever you like as long as you take 30 minutes to write down exactly what you want to change, why you want to change it, and then allow 24 hours before the change takes effect so Pigula can't impulsively convince to eat things for taste or convenience.

- **"Kitchen's Closed!"** As discussed, in the previous

section, one of our Master Coaches claps her hands three times and says, enthusiastically "kitchen's closed!" But this mantra can not only be used to accentuate the demarcation point, it can also be repeated throughout the evening when Pigula bothers you with cravings.

➢ **"I Will Never Binge Again!"** Obviously this brings to mind all the lessons and enthusiastic emotional identification with the first book (free at www.NeverBingeAgain.com)

➢ **"Food is Not for Entertainment."** People who used this mantra wanted to remind themselves that they would not accept the cultural mythology of having to constantly entertain themselves with food, as the Big Food and Big Advertising industries wanted them to think was necessary. Some recalled the idea which I seem to have popularized in my podcasts and previous books that "Every time you look for love at the bottom of a bag, box, or container, there's some fat cat in a white suit with a mustache who's laughing all the way to the bank!"

➢ **"I Will Never Eat Myself to Sleep Again!" Nighttime is for sleeping, and I never eat at night.** Simple but profound.

➢ **"There's NO Amount of Food That Will Satisfy Me at Night So I Choose to Eat Nothing!"** This mantra reflects the painful experience of all too many readers and clients, endured for way too many years. There is a profound and fundamental truth to it for most people. Morning will come, and food will be satisfying once again.

➢ **"Let It Burn!"** Nighttime without overeating is one of the best ways to burn fat. Let it happen. Some people even grab their stomachs, hips, and/or behind when they say this.

While the above mantras have indeed proven effective way beyond the people who initially invented them *(including myself),* it can be even more effective to develop one of your own, very specific to your unique needs and emotional identification. We'll review a procedure for doing so in Part Three.

Last, the above mantras are those which people are successfully utilizing for *evening* cravings. For mantras prove to be more useful during the *daytime,* please see "45 Binge Trigger Busters."

Day Three - Practical Steps

Step 1: Pick a Mantra (or several)

Which of the above mantras particularly appeal to you? Why?

How might you improve the mantra which appeals to you most? Give yourself permission to radically alter it if necessary, in order to customize it for your own needs. Or make up a new one. Regardless, write the very specific mantra you will use when and if Pigula wakes up and attempts to bite you in the evening. Commit to doing this.

If your demarcation line is linked to a very specific time on the clock it can also be extremely useful to set a reminder on your phone so your mantra will pop every night at this time!

Finally, include a copy of your chosen mantra or mantras underneath your written demarcation line rules... not as a rule but as a clear reminder of what to do when you hear Pigula Whispering after "sundown."

Step 2: Revisit and revise your Demarcation Ritual and Decompression Routine as Necessary. Edit the

Never Binge Again Food Rule to Formalize Them as Necessary.

Review last night's experience in writing. How did you do? How did that feel? How did it impact you? What might be changed and/or improved?

Make the changes to the rules if necessary.

CHAPTER 7: NUTRITION AND FOOD ENJOYMENT RULES – OBTAINING THE PHYSICAL AND SPIRITUAL POWERS TO DEFEAT PIGULA

Day Four – Meal Timing and Size Rules

Satisfaction with food during the day helped to curb the nighttime overeating problem dramatically in many of our most successful clients.

We first encountered this idea in a research review by author Jennifer Hand in *Healthline*. Hand suggested when our meals during the day are not satisfying, we are much more likely to overeat late at night (2018). Nighttime overeating may also be "the result of overly restricted daytime food intake, leading to ravenous hunger at night" (West, 2016).

When you are overly cautious of the type and amount of food that you consume throughout the day, you may feel that you are foregoing food satisfaction entirely. This is not a good idea. When what you eat during the day is genuinely satisfying, the idea of overeating after dinner is simply less appealing.

The solution is to find things you can add to your diet to enhance satisfaction without interfering with your health and fitness goals. These often include spices, whole fruit, and/or perhaps small amounts of dark chocolate when you want something sweet *(if you're not someone—like me—who can't have chocolate at all.)* Things which give a satisfying "crunch" during the day like chopped celery on your salad, carrots, cabbage, etc. can also help tremendously. We are meant to bite and chew, and the stress of most of our daily work lives adds to this urge—*this oral aggression can be discharged by more biting and chewing during the day, leaving less of a desire to do so in the evening.*

You might also consider adding dehydrated vegetables as flavor enhancers. For example, a few sundried tomatoes *(without oil and salt)* in your salad can make all the difference in satisfaction and satiation. They also mix very well in soups. And remember, adding a few planned extra calories to your dinner meal is MUCH better than a large amount of spontaneous, unplanned snacking.

Regarding nutrition, we've always warned our clients there are some rules your body will not allow to stand. For example, try adopting a "I Will Never Pee Again" rule and we promise your bladder will force you to ignore it in just a few hours. Similarly, if you don't feed your body adequate nutrition during the day it WILL cry out for more at night. After all, it needs nutritional resources to accomplish its critical evening tasks of rest and regeneration. No matter how strong your intellectual resolve may be, without proper nutrition your brain will work hard to force you to be less discriminating at night because it believes there is a physical emergency.

This is probably why **our most successful clients and readers focused heavily on nutrition during the day.** They'd observed Pigula to Squeal MUCH louder when they were underfed, particularly if they hadn't had a nutritious breakfast, lunch, and dinner.

Now, almost all our clients SAY they have good nutrition, but when you carefully examine the factors in this section with them, you'll almost always find deficiencies. In other words, there no shame in re-examining your nutrition, perhaps especially if you're SURE you're doing fine. Take solace in every deficiency. Each one is an opportunity for improvement that can help nail Pigula's coffin shut at night!

Many successful clients and readers also included a higher-than-average volume of leafy green vegetables throughout the day in their nutritional regimen. And most had either completely eliminated sugar, flour, and other highly processed foods from their diet, or seriously regulated them such that they now played a lesser role.

It was quite noteworthy that without boundaries, very few (if any) nighttime successes were freely eating sugar, flour, and other highly processed and/or industrially concentrated foods. People who successfully overcame Pigula's Squeals were largely avoiding empty calories, **thus ensuring more substantial nutrition during the day**. When they did eat empty calories, they were planned and scripted indulgences with very specific food rules regulating their beginnings and ends. For example, "The only dessert other than whole fruit I will ever eat again is one serving from the menu at a restaurant no more than one day per calendar week."

Some people also included more protein with their dinner to prevent hunger during the night. And many planned out *(or even prepared)* their dinners in the morning, ensuring they'd have the necessary ingredients, and eliminating the need to make any decisions at night when they knew they'd be fatigued and short on willpower.

Then there was the timing of the meals. Many successful clients said a hearty breakfast, a medium lunch, and a lighter but very nutritious dinner made it MUCH easier to stop at their designated cut off time.

Science seems to suggest the "breakfast like a king, lunch like a prince, and dinner like a pauper" philosophy may be a good way to fight our natural tendency to crave more sweet, starchy, and salty foods in the evening. These evolutionary cravings may have served us well during a time when industrially concentrated foods were not an option—*there were NO potato chips, pizza, chocolate, etc. in the tropics 100,000 years ago*—but in modern times these urges lead us astray. Here's a quick review of the more pertinent research:

> A study conducted by Sato-Mite et al. suggests dividing the population into "morning-types" and "evening-types" (Harb et al., 2012). The result of several studies reviewed by these researchers was that "evening-types tend to skip breakfast more", and morning-types who wake up earlier are MUCH more able to have discipline in diet control (Harb et al., 2012).
>
> Researchers at Harvard University published a study in the journal Obesity which further explains the role our biology has on our late-night overeating habits. They found "an internal circadian rhythm causes increased appetite in the evening" (OHSU News, 2013). They speculate that overeating at later hours may have previously served our ancestors to "store energy to survive longer in times of food scarcity," but that in today's age, it has promoted un-

healthy eating habits (OHSU News, 2013).

A similar study discussed in the Obesity suggests that our body's internal clock increases hunger and cravings for sweet, starchy and salty foods in the evenings. Subjects in this study felt "least hungry in the morning," at about 8 A.M., and "most hungry" at around 8 P.M. The authors suggest our appetites' internal circadian regulation leaves us with a "natural tendency to skip breakfast in favor of larger meals in the evening," an eating routine ever-more common in modern times (OHSU News, 2013). Skipping breakfast and overeating late at night starts a vicious habit, which can easily become a full-blown eating disorder such as NES.

A study (Karatzi et al., 2017) published in the journal "Nutrition" found that "late-night overeating is associated with fewer calories consumed at breakfast *and* with breakfast skipping". They observed that a cycle developed which included skipping breakfast, overeating at dinner, and snacking late at night which created a stubborn trend in an individuals' eating schedule. When an individual skips breakfast, they mitigate the low-calorie intake through other meals during their day, which, in turn, can disrupt their mealtimes and motivate them to have an earlier lunch and dinner.

While the individual may not be concerned about their daytime mealtimes, having an earlier dinner can create the opportunity *(and urge)* for a <u>*second*</u> dinner and/or a late-night high-calorie and/or high-volume snack. Then, the nighttime overeating causes their "stomach to expand [...] to adjust to the large amount of food," and more hydrochloric acid is required to break it down, which can make them feel bloated and disinterested in eating in the morning. Thus, the cycle is reset and perpetuated, and in the long-term can cause heartburn, insomnia, and obesity. Un-

> fortunately, the "slowed digestive process means the food you eat will remain in the stomach for a longer period of time and be more likely to turn into fat" (Blackburn, 2018).

In sum, like your Momma said, don't skip breakfast. Skipping breakfast is a strong contributor to the nighttime overeating pattern!

Many of our most successful clients had also decided to move their dinner to later in the evening. They reasoned they'd become ravenous late at night because they were attempting to fast for too long between dinner and breakfast. A later dinner and an earlier breakfast bridged that gap and made it easier to keep Pigula in its Coffin at night. Lunch for the later-dinner clients was also a little later in the day to make it easier to wait. So, the pattern was early breakfast, mid-afternoon lunch, and a later dinner... but not so late that you'll have trouble wanting to eat breakfast in the morning.

Although you can customize this for your individual needs, a typical success pattern might include a substantial breakfast no later than 8 am, a satisfying and filling lunch around 1:30 or 2:00 pm, and highly nutritious but somewhat less substantial dinner at 7 or 7:30 pm.

EAT A HEARTY BREAKFAST, A MEDIUM LUNCH, AND A LIGHTER BUT VERY NUTRITIOUS DINNER!

> "Well... That's that, you hate eating breakfast, we can't possibly implement this in our lives, so let's just skip all this nonsense and go buy stuff for our nightly binge" – Count Pigula

Well...

NO!!!

By now you know that if you can't follow the scientific advice to the letter, you can improvise and create a routine that achieves 95% of the benefits while STILL keeping releasing Pigula in its coffin.

For example, if you can't have a hearty breakfast, you can have a quick bite before you leave home and then a quick meal at 9 am or 10 am.

For example, Yoav (my co-author), swims most days in the morning. So instead of having a hearty breakfast which he says his stomach won't be able to contain during the hour-long swimming workout, he has a few crackers before he leaves the house. Then, when he's done with his workout, he has a larger meal—usually a sandwich or a protein shake with a Banana. This way he gets eats substantially during the morning even though he can't have a hearty "breakfast."

Then, there's some evidence that indulging in food-sensitive substances during the day may contribute to night-time binges. Find and eliminate your food sensitivities. Some very common ones I've seen make a very significant difference with clients are gluten and dairy.

Another interesting research tidbit is that Vitamin D helps regulate blood sugar at night, and if you're deficient this may be a reason for cravings. Ask your doctor to check your levels and let you know whether you need to supplement with Vitamin D. *(Be safe with the sun).*

Yet another important distinction between people who overcame nighttime overeating and those who did not was that those who "counted points" *(calories, program points, etc.)* paid particular attention to *finishing* their points during the day.

They found this made evening cravings a lot less likely. In other words, **avoid the temptation to leave points over for evening (to indulge)**.

Finally, many successful clients planned out their dinner in the morning before leaving for the day. Some even prepared it and set it aside in the refrigerator in prepackaged containers of Tupperware. As you'll discover in the next section on self-care, this can work wonders by eliminating nighttime food decisions. Since our willpower is weakest in the evening, this eliminated the need to rely upon it for difficult nighttime decisions. It set them up for success. *"I pack all my meals in the morning, eat outside the house, and then come home to an activity I was looking forward to doing. I think having a good plan and not having to make any food decision works for me."*

SUMMARY OF SUCCESSFUL NUTRITIONAL ADJUSTMENTS FOR NIGHTTIME OVEREATERS

➢ **Most importantly, try to enhance your satisfaction with food during the day.** Consider adding more "hard chew" foods like carrots, celery, cabbage, etc. Dehydrated vegetables may also add flavor and contribute to satiation and satisfaction. For those who don't lose control with dark chocolate, a few squares after lunch or dinner may do the trick. *(But please use with caution as many of my readers find the intensity of pleasure from dark chocolate to be too much for them to resist and they subsequently decide to abandon restraint entirely)*

➢ Emphasize hearty breakfast, medium sized lunch, and a reasonably light but ultra-nutritious dinner.

➢ Move dinner later in the evening and breakfast earlier in the morning to create fewer fasting hours at night. Consider including protein in your evening meal to keep you full longer.

➢ Try to eat lunch a little later than you normally do in order to create a shorter wait between lunch and dinner. This will further encourage you to eat a substantial breakfast.

➢ If not medically contraindicated, and if in concert with your Never Binge Again dietary philosophy, be sure to include plenty of leafy green vegetables during the day, and enough protein in your evening meal to keep you satiated.

➢ Examine your overall nutrition with a licensed dietitian, or, at minimum, review a full week's consumption with one of the online nutrition and calorie calculators like Cronometer.com or MyFitnessPal.com. Especially if you THINK you have your nutrition covered! *(Many clients who struggle at night were very surprised when they actually calculated the results)*

➢ Consider a slower weight loss pace. Caloric and nutritional deficiencies create significant binge urges.

➢ Make sure you're not deficient in Vitamin D, which reportedly helps regulate blood sugar in the evening. Ask your doctor how to test and address this please.

➢ If you count points of any kind, try to finish them by dinnertime. Avoid the temptation to leave points over for evening.

➢ Plan out (and even prepare) your evening meals in the morning before leaving for work. Set everything aside so it's just waiting for you when you get home, and you know it will be all day while you're out.

Nutrition and Nighttime Overeating References

Blackburn, K. B. (2018, February). What happens when you overeat? Retrieved from https://www.mdanderson.org/publications/focused-on-health/What-happens-when-you-overeat.h23Z1592202.html

Harb, A., Levandovski, R., Oliveira, C., Caumo, W., Allison, K. C., Stunkard, A., & Hidalgo, M. P. (2012). Night eating patterns and chronotypes: A correlation with binge eating behaviors. *Psychiatry Research,200*(2-3), 489-493. doi:10.1016/j.psychres.2012.07.004

Hand, J. (n.d.). Binge Eating at Night? Here's How To Stop [Web log post]. Retrieved from https://www.mindbodygreen.com/articles/the-3-things-you-need-to-do-to-stop-over-eating-at-night

Hyman, M. "8 Steps to Stop Your Nighttime Binges." [Blog post. Retrieved from https://drhyman.com/blog/2013/10/09/8-steps-stop-nighttime-binges/]

OHSU News. (2013, April 29). Study explains what triggers those late-night snack cravings. Retrieved from https://news.ohsu.edu/2013/04/29/study-explains-what-triggers-those-late-night-snack-cravings

Sass, C. (2017, January 31). The Surprising Reason You Snack at Night (and How to Stop It). Retrieved from https://www.health.com/obesity/the-surprising-reason-you-snack-at-night-and-how-to-stop-it

West, H. (2016, June 21). 10 Clever Ways to Stop Eating Late at Night. Retrieved from https://www.healthline.com/nutrition/10-ways-to-stop-eating-late-at-night

Day Four – Practical Steps

Step 1: Take Stock of Your Meal Timing and Size

How long, on average, do you try to go without eating from your last bite in the evening until your first bite the next day? What's been your best thinking regarding this goal? Put the answers in writing and be sure you know why you're doing what you're doing. Remember, the most essential thing you can do with food to overcome nighttime overeating is enhance *daytime* food satisfaction.

The timing and size of your meals can also make a big difference, but provided you're getting enough calories and nutrition during the day, you don't necessarily need to change anything about this. *(If I had my druthers, I'd still get everyone who struggles with the nighttime eating issue to eat a reasonable breakfast at or before 8 am, and move their dinner an hour or so later than they've been accustomed to in order to create a shorter fasting window between dinner and breakfast. But if this rubs you the wrong way, please know it's entirely optional.)*

Step 2: Plan your meals

Is there ANY way you'd be comfortable having an earlier breakfast, or becoming a breakfast eater if you've not been one to this date? And is there any way you could move some calories you generally eat later in the day to your morning meal? Write down specifically how you plan to implement this.

Do you need to add more vegetables, fruit, protein or fat to your meals? If you're deficient in one of these categories, your body will constantly "feel deprived."

It's also particularly important to look forward to the morning meal. So, what might you add to your breakfast to make it more enjoyable without seriously interfering with your health and fitness goals?

Write down how your meal plan will play out in different circumstances. How and when will you eat on a regular day at work vs. the weekends at home? What about when you're traveling and/or at family functions and social events? Remember to account for food availability. Plan to diversify your eating so you won't get bored repeatedly eating the same meals.

This task might take you a few hours, but by the time you're done you'll have achieved a new level of clarity and confidence in your ability to Pigula away for good.

Step 3: Add rules to your food plan that support your planned meal timing and sizes

This is where the rubber meets the road. Add specific Never Binge Again *rules (as described in chapter 5)* which support the changes you've committed to implementing above. Examples:

- I always review my food plan for the coming week on Sundays and buy whatever is required in order to prepare my meals for the week.
- I will never again go to sleep before planning my meals for the next day.
- I will never again go to sleep on weekdays before packing my 10 am meal AND lunch for the next day.
- I will always have a protein bar before leaving the house for the first time in the morning, and a sandwich <u>*without*</u> fatty-meats and/or cheeses from the deli closest to my office at 10 am.

- I will never again skip breakfast even when I am not hungry!

The idea here is to create realistic rules you can follow, but which will also change the way you eat so you get adequate nutrition and satisfaction from your food during the day. For example, eating a protein bar before leaving the house and then a sandwich at the deli is not *(by any means)* the healthiest way to eat, but if you don't have time to prepare breakfast then this will be 100 times better than skipping it altogether and then letting Pigula go to town at night!

Be creative. Create the best rules for yourself and when nighttime comes, you'll have more than enough strength to resist Pigula!

Day FIVE – Add Some Crunch to Your Lunch!

What's Your "Lunch-Crunch" Level? Are you crunching enough during the day? Take stock of what you're eating that requires you to actually CHEW. Industrially softened foods like bread and bagels don't count, nor does artificially enhanced crunching like that found in chips, etc. What foods in their natural form are you crunching on during the day? How often are you eating them and how much satisfaction are you deriving from them? Pay particular attention to the afternoon meal but remember to evaluate dinner too.

Day Five – Practical Steps

Step 1: Add More Crunch to Your Lunch

Write down two specific ingredients you can occasionally add to your meal in order to enhance your lunch-crunch enjoyment. Most obvious would be things like carrots, celery, zucchini, cucumbers, and/or cruciferous vegetables like broccoli and cauliflower to your salads, and/or using them with one of the delicious dips in the recipes section of this book. But have you considered things like peapods, jicama, apples, pears, whole sugar cane in its natural form *(not the juice or refined sugar),* almonds, cashews, and sunflower seeds? Of course, you'll need to be careful with the calories from nuts and seeds, best utilized in small volumes.

The trick is not necessarily eating these crunch-enhancers alone, but as part of a meal and/or salad where they can absorb a tasty dressing or sauce. Take note of a few recipes if that helps you.

Plan to include more crunch in your lunch at least two days this week. Go shopping to be sure you have the ingredients. Then mark your plans on your calendar. Extra credit if you add some crunch to your dinner too! And we promise not to call the crunch police on you if you go beyond two days a week.

Step 2: Define Never Binge Again Rules to Guarantee You Get Your Crunch

These should be very simple rules to create. Examples:

- I will always eat two cucumbers at lunch when I'm eating at home.
- I will always ask for an extra serving of uncooked carrots, celery, or cucumbers when eating out.

But wait... is this the voice of Pigula we hear again?

Why yes, it is!

> "Now they want us to have crunch rules. I told you, these guys are crazy. Just put this silly book down and let's have a good ol' feast, what do you say buddy? Pleaaasssssseeee..."
> – Your "Buddy" Pigula

Well...

As usual, Pigula is using a half-truth to convince you to break the seal on its coffin and convince you to destroy your health and self-esteem for a little "food fun."

Pigula is half-right because crunch rules ARE second tier rules, which means you can actually do extremely well *without* them. If you don't like crunchy food, or it'll be a hassle to add these types of foods to your meals then you COULD skip the crunch rules entirely.

But, adding even just the occasional supplemental crunch to your meals can make a big different. Perhaps you could create rules to govern the specific occasions? For example:

- I always add two cucumbers to my plate when they happen to be available at home.
- I always pack an apple for lunchtime when I leave the house.

But here's Pigula going at it again...

> "You know, one day you'll forget to pack that apple, and I'll come right out of my cage and rule your life forever, muhahahahaha! So, let's just skip the nonsense and go straight for the cookies!" - Pigula

We've already discussed this Pigula whisper, but it's worth dissecting again...

1. You are not making a plan to forget, you are making a plan to remember, Pigula would like you to plan to forget, but you can easily set reminders on your phone. Put a note on the door that says "remember the apple" and so on.
2. If you do forget *(which MAY happen a few times at first),* that doesn't mean you'll let Pigula out, it only means that you'll be slightly miffed with yourself, and perhaps you'll need to adjust your plan and queues to better remind you of the apple.
3. Pigula's Whispers are always meant to get you to eat junk RIGHT NOW. They are never really about later. The urge to eat NOW because of a "mistake" you've made is a clear indication Pigula is whispering in your ear. Listen carefully for a few seconds and you'll see the false logic it's attempting to use to convince you. Just bring yourself back to the present moment and say "Shut up Pigula and go back to your coffin! I never break my rules NOW, and since it will always be NOW, I will never break my rules again!"

Day Six – Daytime Flavor Enhancement

Study the Principles of Healthy Flavor Enhancement

Educate yourself about these simple flavor enhancement principles so you can creatively begin to add to the enjoyment of your daytime meals without too many extra calories and/or interfering with your health and fitness goals.

- **Proper Use of Herbs**: Hardier herbs like rosemary, sage, thyme, and marjoram are better added to your meal earlier in the cooking process so they can release maximum flavor while simultaneously developing a less abrasive texture. More delicate herbs like chives, cilantro, parsley, and basil are better added last minute.

➢ **Higher Quality Condiments**: Consider some high-quality condiment choices like wasabi, bean puree, flavored mustard, salsa, horseradish, etc. Use them when you marinate and cook for extra flavor, or after your meal is prepared to add some extra hot kick to your dish.

➢ **Lemon Juice and Red Wine Vinegar**: If you want to add some extra flavor to your dish without adding salt, butter, and/or oil you can consider acidic edibles like lemon juice, red wine vinegar, orange juice, limes, etc. If you're going to use citrus, make sure it's fresh. Citrus loses its vibrancy —especially in juice form—when it sits around too long. This can actually detract from the flavor of your dish making it taste duller and flatter. But fresh citrus is amazing!

➢ **Use Spices and Grind Them Fresh When You Can**: If you can occasionally afford the time to grind your own spices, you'll find them to be more flavorful, especially if you toast them in a dry skillet first. But even if you can't, some ginger, turmeric, habanero (and other) peppers, coriander, paprika, nutmeg, cinnamon, cumin, cardamom, cloves, etc., added to *your* taste *(carefully at first)*, can make ALL the difference in your dish. It's important to throw out your old spices, and then to clean and consolidate them in your cabinet so you're both very conscious of your spice inventory and eager to utilize them whenever you can.

➢ **Do Not Remove the Seeds from Tomatoes**: Don't deseed a tomato before you cook with it and/or put it in a salad. The seed is where most of the flavor lives!

➢ **Garlic**: Vampires hate garlic, need we say more? Garlic becomes hotter and more pungent the more finely you chop it up. Grating it on a grater or crushing it in a press creates much finer particles than hand-chopping, further strengthening the flavor. Combining garlic with a little sea salt and crushing it with a mortar and pestle produces the most intense garlic flavor – usually too intense for all but the most avid garlic lovers, or to really enhance the flavor of a salad dressing. If you want the sweetness and aroma of garlic without the heat you can throw it in the microwave for 30 seconds before you use it. This deactivates the enzymes that trigger the "hot" garlic flavor. According to Chef Kenji Lopez-Alt, combining raw garlic with heated garlic in a dish produces the most interesting complexity of flavors of all. "A single dish with slow-cooked whole cloves along with some sautéed sliced garlic and just a bit of raw grated garlic at the end fires on all of its garlicky cylinders" he says (Lopez-Alt, 2017).

Also, for the most health benefits from Allicin *(the immune boosting and cancer fighting factor in garlic)* always use fresh garlic, not bottled. Garlic in water loses half its Allicin in six days, whereas garlic stored in oil loses that much in just three hours! Also, to maximize the formation of Allicin compounds, cut the garlic and wait 10 to 15 minutes before cooking. This allows the compounds to form before heat inactivates the enzymes.

To get rid of garlic breath, floss your teeth and/or chew on some parsley.

➢ **Roasting Vegetables**: You can add a tremendous amount of flavor to your dishes without adding many calories if you add some roasted vegetables. It's NOT at all necessary to coat your vegetables with oil when you roast them in the oven. It takes a little longer to achieve the color and texture you're accustomed to, but it can and will happen. Root vegetables such as potatoes, parsnips, sweet potatoes and carrots are some of the best vegetables to roast.

➢ **Dehydrating Vegetables**: If you're not a fan of roasting you can also dehydrate your vegetables. Chop up a bunch of celery and put it in the blender. Then spread it out with a spatula on the parchment paper to go in your dehydrator. Dehydrate it for about 24 hours at 115 degrees, then peel it off the paper and put it back in the blender *(better yet, a coffee grinder)* and you'll have made "celery salt." Celery salt has no sodium chloride and reportedly doesn't affect your blood pressure, yet you shouldn't miss your regular table salt. *(Thanks to my friend Jena for teaching me this.)* This is just one of the many things you can do with a dehydrator. Making "sun dried" tomatoes is another. Adding just a few to your salad can make all the difference in taste and satiation. But pretty much any vegetable you can eat, you can dehydrate to concentrate the flavor!

➢ **Dehydrating Fruits**: Used carefully, dehydrated fruits can add a tremendous amount of flavor to your dishes. Even just a few raisins, dehydrated blueberries, strawberries, etc. can turn a boring salad into a more enjoyable meal. And there are all sorts of reasonably healthy deserts you can make with dehydrated bananas, dates, etc. But because they are very caloric, use with caution. Not everyone can eat dehydrated fruit – know yourself first.

References:

➢ Lifehacker (2014, October 23rd). "10 Simple Tips to Make Food Taste Better." Retrieved from https://lifehacker.com/ten-simple-tips-to-make-food-taste-better-1649821924

➢ Vanner, C. (2018, March 20th). "The Best Ways to Make Your Food More Flavorful." Retrieved from https://www.forkly.com/food-hacks/20-ways-to-make-your-food-more-flavorful/

➢ Lopez-Alt, K. (2017, January 30th). "Help Me, Kenji – How to Maximize Garlic Flavor." Retrieved from https://www.cookinglight.com/cooking-101/help-me-kenji-how-to-maximize-garlic-flavor

➢ Obrien, D. (Date not published). "4 Tips for Cooking with Garlic." Retrieved from http://www.eatingwell.com/article/275955/4-tips-for-how-to-cook-with-garlic/

Day Six – Practical Steps

Step 1: Review at least one meal you've eaten since you began the 10-Day Challenge and make a plan for enhancing its flavor using the principles above.

Plan to incorporate that meal into tomorrow's food. Take the time to breathe before you eat. Relish the meal. Thoroughly enjoy and let it both satisfy and nourish you. *(NOTE: You won't lose any points, and I promise not to send the food-satisfaction police after you if you work on more than one meal. But try to do at least one!)*

Step 2: Optionally add NBA Flavor rules to your food plan

For example:

- I will always add mustard to my sandwich.
- I will always add sun-dried tomatoes to my salad (when available)
- Etc'

Step 3: (For advanced practitioners) - Review all your meals and add flavor to each of your standard dishes

This is a bit of work but can change your life completely! Not only will you be happier with the food you eat every time you sit down for a meal, you'll quickly discover that Pigula has become a lot quieter at night because you've robbed it of its best argument: You no longer feel deprived!

> "Adding flavor... What are they thinking?!?! ... Wait... That's actually not a bad idea... We love flavors...I'm confused"
>
> Pigula :-(

CHAPTER 8: YOUR PILLOW – THE SILVER CROSS

There are a variety of studies which suggest "staying up late, during hours you should be sleeping increases the odds of overeating at night" *(Sass, 2017; Harb et al., 2012).* The majority of clients and readers who overcame nighttime overeating also said they'd moved their bedtime at least a little earlier:

➢ "I don't let myself wander around the kitchen when I should be asleep!" was a common refrain.

➢ "If I can't sleep, at minimum I'll stay in bed with movies and books."

➢ "I avoid staying up alone at all costs – it almost always leads to a food binge"

➢ "I never stay up past 11 pm. I'll begin to get hungry again if I'm awake for too many hours beyond my evening my meal."

➢ Other previous nighttime eaters reported that if cravings became very bad, they'd go to sleep as early as 8 pm. "If I'm tempted, I go take a bath or go to bed early. If I go to bed really early, sometimes I'll wake up the next day really early, but that's ok because I'm not tempted to binge in the morning."

Furthermore, many successfully recovered nighttime overeaters emphasized the sanctity of the bedroom for sleep and/or intimacy with a "no eating in a sleeping room" rule.

Finally, getting enough sleep is critical. Sleep deprivation and fatigue tend to increase levels of ghrelin, the "let's eat" hormone. In fact, people who get 4 or fewer hours of sleep per night may consume as much as 22% more calories per day on average!

References – Early Bedtime as an Aid to Stop Nighttime Overeating

➢ Sass, C. (2017, January 31). The Surprising Reason You Snack at Night (and How to Stop It). Retrieved from https://www.health.com/obesity/the-surprising-reason-you-snack-at-night-and-how-to-stop-it

➢ Harb, A., Levandovski, R., Oliveira, C., Caumo, W., Allison, K. C., Stunkard, A., & Hidalgo, M. P. (2012). Night eating patterns and chronotypes: A correlation with binge eating behaviors. *Psychiatry Research,200*(2-3), 489-493. doi:10.1016/j.psychres.2012.07.004

➢ Blay, Libby. (2016, September 9th). [Blog post]. Retrieved from https://fitmo.com/personal-trainer-blog/stop-food-cravings-tired-hungry/

Day Seven – Earlier Bedtime

What time do you currently retire to bed for the evening? How do you feel about that time? Would it bother you to move it 30 to 60 minutes earlier? Why or why not? What might be good about it? What might be bad about it? How might you problem solve your concerns?

Journal about this in detail please.

Today might also be a good time to ask Pigula why going to sleep early is a really stupid and evil idea. It will likely say things like...

> "But we love staying up at night ~~stuffing our pie-holes~~ (I'm sorry, ignore that) - thinking, having time to ourselves, watching movies, reading, relaxing – are we really going to give up our favorite time of the day?"

Or...

> "There's no way this is going to work, we're night owls, we just won't fall asleep and then we'll get bored and eat even more"

Write down every objection Pigula raises, then calmly identify the half-truths and false logic in each statement. This is a great way to strengthen your refutation-muscle, the one you use to nullify Pigula's arguments. If you're having a problem refuting any yourself, you can always head over to our forum and ask our community for help. *(http://www.NeverBingeAgainForum.com)*

Day Seven - Practical Steps

Step 1: Determine your bedtime

Most nighttime overeaters don't even have a fixed bedtime, they just go to bed whenever they feel like it *(often after a pretty gruesome binge).* Therefore, your first step is to simply decide when you'd like bedtime to be.

Step 2: Make an NBA rule about your bedtime

Going to bed earlier can be extremely helpful for nighttime overeaters. At the same time, we know it's a difficult habit to initiate. So instead of thinking of this as a lifetime rule, for now, just commit to a 10-day experiment. You can decide whether you want and/or need to keep the earlier bedtime based upon the evidence of this experiment.

But whether you decide to make this a 10-day or a lifelong habit, create a new NBA rule and add it to your food plan. For example, "I will always turn off the TV and go to bed by 10 pm."

Day Eight – Get Better Sleep

There's no doubt about it. An abundance of evidence suggests poor sleep immediately effects your brain function, sports performance, and hormones. It also contributes to weight gain and increased risk of serious diseases across the age spectrum. On the other hand, good sleep helps you to eat and exercise better, and lowers your risks for a wide variety of health issues.

Unfortunately sleep length and quality has been on the decline in our modern world for several decades. Thankfully, there are many evidence-based approaches you can integrate into your life to improve your sleep, and several of them work in short order:

➢ **Stop caffeine intake after 3 pm.** Caffeine can stay in your blood for six to eight hours. Need I say more?

➢ **Increase your exposure to sunlight and/or sunlight replacements.** This is proven to help balance your hormones and tell your body when it's time to be awake vs. sleeping. There's evidence that as little as two hours of bright light exposure can reduce the time it takes to fall asleep by up to 83% and increase your average amount of sleep by up to two hours. We are clearly meant to spend time outside every day, but if you can't, consider investing in an artificial bright light device to use indoors. It's a big deal.

➢ **Use lower lighting during your Decompression Time:** This will further enhance your body's perception sleep is coming, and that it's time to "let go of the day."

➢ **Turn off your screens!** The blue light exposure you receive from your smart phone, tablet, and computer negatively impacts your circadian rhythm and tricks your brain into thinking it's still daytime. Not good! But if you're just too addicted to your gadgets and don't want to give them up, there are apps that block blue light for your smartphone, tablet, or computer. Search your App Store for "blue light" apps. You can also buy a special pair of glasses to use for this purpose. Google "blue light glasses" to find them.

➢ **Reduce noise and light in the bedroom environment.** These can cause poor sleep and long-term health issues.

➢ **Stick to consistent sleep and wake times.** Being consistent with sleep times is shown to significantly increase long term sleep quality, and irregular sleep patterns can confuse your circadian rhythm, making you think you should be awake when you should be sleeping. Ideally this means you go to bed at the same time on the weekends as you do during the week. I know that's not always practical, you should know where the bullseye is because, like my grandfather always said "if you don't know what you're aiming for you'll probably hit something else!"

➢ **Get some exercise during the day – NOT before bed.** This can improve all aspects of sleep, especially in older adults. Ask your doctor if it's OK first.

➢ **Melatonin.** Ask your doctor if melatonin may be a helpful way for you to fall asleep faster, stay asleep longer, and wake feeling more refreshed.

➢ **Stop drinking liquids a few hours before bed.** Less peeing = more sleeping, yah?

➢ **Get a more comfortable mattress.** Studies suggest it can not only improve back and shoulder pain, but significantly enhance sleep quality.

➢ **Other Supplements:** Several other supplements are reported to help with relaxation and sleep induction. These include Valerian Root, Magnesium, L-Theanine, and Lavender. Check with your doctor to see if these may help.

➢ **Cut down (or cut out) the alcohol.** Alcohol increases disrupted sleep patterns, alters nighttime melatonin production, interferes with your body's natural tendency to elevate Human Growth Hormone in the evening, and thereby also disrupts your circadian rhythm.

➢ **Find the right temperature for your bedroom.** It's more difficult to get a good night's sleep if it's too warm or too cold. Experiment and find the right temperature for you. Write it down so you don't forget.

➢ **Adopt a relaxation or meditation routine to help you wind down.** There are dozens of smart phone applications to help you with this. My favorite is "Relax Melodies." Calm.com will also work on your computer.

➢ **Incorporate a warm bath or shower into your Demarcation Ritual and/or Decompression Time.** A multitude of studies suggest this can help us fall asleep and significantly improve sleep quality, especially as we age.

➢ **See your doctor.** If all the above are ineffective at helping you to improve the quality of your sleep, consider getting tested for a sleep disorder. Especially amongst overweight people, sleep apnea *(difficulty breathing while sleeping)* is common. There are also a variety of other disorders and conditions which can interfere with sleep that require medical treatment. Alzheimer's Disease is a special case, for example. So are movement disorders like Restless Leg's Syndrome *(the sensation of tingling, crawling, and "pins and needles" when you lay down at night).*

➢ **Avoid activities that "keep you up at night"** – If, for example, talking to your mother or going out with friends cause you to toss and turn all night, it's better you perform these activities earlier in the day.

➢ **Perform activities that relax you before bedtime** – If, for example, knitting or reading autobiographies of world leaders makes you drowsy, turn off the TV 15 minutes earlier and do those activities then. This can be a great way to relax your mind and put you in a sleepy state.

Sleep References

➢ US Department of Health and Human Services. "A Good Night's Sleep." Retrieved from https://www.nia.nih.gov/health/good-nights-sleep

➢ Mower, R. (2018, November 2nd). "17 Proven Tips for Better Sleep". Retrieved from https://www.healthline.com/nutrition/17-tips-to-sleep-better

➢ Harvard Medical (2017, December 18th). "Twelve Simple Tips to Improve your Sleep." Retrieved from http://healthysleep.med.harvard.edu/healthy/getting/overcoming/tips

Day Eight – Practical Steps

Step 1: Plan your sleep improvement

Take stock of the above sleep improvement opportunities. Which ones are you already implementing, which ones may be of interest? What resistance might you feel to implementing at least one more, and how might your Pigula be responsible for that resistance? Write it down please.

Step 2: Put the plan into action

➢ Create a Never Binge Again rule for implementing at least one sleep improvement technique from the above list.

➢ Evaluate yesterday's bedtime change, if any, and adjust as you see fit.

CHAPTER 9: SELF CARE – YOUR PERSONAL HOLY WATER

Day Nine – Self Care Rules

When we first began seeing Never Binge Again clients who struggled with nighttime overeating, we found virtually all were deficient in self-care and self-nurturance during the day. They all seemed to feel like they weren't entitled to and/or didn't deserve to take more time for these activities. This, in turn, empowered Pigula to say something like "Oh C'mon, there's at least ONE little pleasure we deserve to indulge in today, let's go get some!" And this Whisper was very appealing for these clients because they genuinely hadn't had enough pleasure during the day.

The hardest part of our job was convincing clients this *was* the case. Most believed they were already putting more than enough time into self-love and self-nurturance, but their nighttime eating didn't budge until we added more! Admittedly this was before we had researched all the other factors involved in nighttime overeating, so we were only focused on this one pillar, but still, the finding left a very significant impression on us. It's like there were a million little demons on our clients' shoulders saying "don't even consider that!" We had to work exceptionally hard to pull those demons off.

See, the idea you need more self-care is a little crazy-making and hard to believe at first, and if your instinct says "this doesn't apply to me", you're probably exactly the kind of person we're targeting with this message.

Anyway, there is a significant *(though now slightly controversial)* body of research suggesting that willpower isn't some genetic gift or fixed talent certain people have and other people don't. Rather, it's said to be more like a muscle which is depleted largely by decision making, but also by fatigue, lack of sleep, low blood sugar, stress, and other negative events during the day. There are apparently only so many good decisions we can make each day.

In other words, willpower is kind of like gas in your tank. You're always burning it as you encounter stressful decisions while move through your day, but you can replenish it using various types of self-care and mood elevation techniques.

It's important to realize that even non-food decisions will tax your willpower. People have trouble resisting marshmallows, for example, after they are asked to do difficult math problems. And every time you process an email you must DECIDE whether it requires your response, should be delegated, deferred, reported as spam, etc. These micro-decisions ALL take their toll!

We can use our knowledge about self-care to both bolster our willpower at night by adding a few replenishment breaks throughout our day, and to set ourselves up for success by *eliminating food decisions at night* to when possible.

If you struggle with nighttime overeating, make your food decisions for the day early in the morning, when you're fresh. If you have the time, you can even prepare your dinner in the morning, and leave it waiting for you in some Tupperware in the refrigerator before you head out for the day. *(If that is the one activity that will determine your success, create an NBA rule for it!)*

On a practical basis we've found it makes a difference in nighttime eating struggles when we can get clients to add even two x five-minute breaks during their day. But the more self-care you can add, the better. If you feel you don't deserve and/or won't/can't take time for self-care—*meditation, exercise, baths, journaling, naps, etc*—your body may fight back with rising cortisol levels, which will upset your sleep and hunger patterns, creating a vicious cycle.

What type of self-care are we talking about?

- Walking
- Journaling
- Baths
- Yoga
- Psychotherapy
- Writing down at least one good thing that happened every day
- Meditation / Guided Visualizations
- Deep Breathing
- Aromatherapy
- Listen to Music
- Watch/Listen to Comedy
- Chamomile Tea

- Routines (even vacuuming – anything regular)
- Take an afternoon off *(turn off cell phone, computer, etc)*
- Focusing on just ONE thing to worry about and insisting that you write down at least one potential solution, plus a plan for the worst-case scenario.
- Avoiding people who bother you wherever possible
- Eat That Frog! (Brian Tracy). This refers to tackling the most difficult and bothersome task on your list first and foremost every day.
- Use the ABCDE method for managing tasks and managing overwhelm *(A = Must Do, B = Should Do, C = Nice to Do, D = Delegate, E = Eliminate)*
- Napping
- Get More Hugs
- Spend Time with Pets
- Doing Some Art
- Kissing
- Call a Friend
- Short Exercise Bursts *(Even Two Minutes Long)*
- Prayer
- B-Vitamin Rich Foods *(leafy greens, avocados, broccoli)*
- Prepare for the day tomorrow ahead of time in writing
- Manage your budget to eliminate financial stress
- Review a past success in detail

- Shift your focus of control – avoid powerless statements
- Take control of your surroundings *(drive BEFORE rush hour, etc)*
- Learn to say NO!
- Get Outside (for even 5 minutes)

And then there's sleep! The body can confuse the need for sleep with the need for food. The inhibitory abilities of your neocortex are also diminished when sleep deprived. Your hormonal balance—including hunger hormones—is disturbed, and studies suggest sleep deprivation may cause us to seek 22% more calories during the day than people who get a full night's rest. Also, without sufficient sleep your goals and dreams seem less important, including your weight loss, health, and fitness goals.

Plus, just as it's necessary to at least somewhat enjoy your food during the day in order to mitigate nighttime cravings, it's also necessary to have at least some FUN each day! Make time to integrate fun, relaxation, and other types of pleasure into your life. You not only deserve it, it's part of your "job" as an adult in this world so you can have what it takes to care for others too. Try to do at least one of these things at NIGHT before bed. Otherwise Pigula will say "The only good thing in life is overeating and junk." And why give that vile creature extra ammunition?

Finally, studies indicate the more stress you experience during the day, the more important it is to incorporate additional self-care. Unfortunately, the more stress you experience, the more you will *believe* there is no time. It's critical you remind yourself these feelings aren't facts. Everyone can insert a few five-minute breaks during the day. This should not only reduce cravings in the evening and preserve your willpower but reduce your experience of stress during the day!

Using the vampire metaphor, we like to think of self-care as your personal "Holy Water."

Holy water does not appear in folklore or mythology as a vampire killer nearly as frequently as the silver cross. However, modern filmmakers have eagerly adopted it in very creative ways. In the movies and on television, holy water can burn a vampire's skin like acid, or severely poison the creature if ingested. One of the most creative uses of holy water—and the one we found most useful for our purposes—was in Stephen King's "Salem's Lot."

In Salem's Lot holy water was utilized as a detection device. It would light up and glow when vampires were present, foreshadowing a potentially dangerous encounter so that the main characters could take appropriate actions. This is an apt metaphor. If you monitor your self-care during the day and recognize when it's dropping below critical levels, this can predict Pigula's potential appearance in the evening. Take appropriate action and prepare!

References for Self-Care, Ego Depletion, and Willpower

- ➢ Baumeister, R. F.; Bratslavsky, E.; Muraven, M.; Tice, D. M. (1998). "Ego depletion: Is the active self a limited resource?" (PDF). Journal of Personality and Social Psychology. 74(5): 1252–1265. CiteSeerX 10.1.1.353.2704. doi:10.1037/0022-3514.74.5.1252. PMID 959944

- ➢ Baumeister, Roy F. (2002-04-01). "Ego Depletion and Self-Control Failure: An Energy Model of the Self's Executive Function". Self and Identity. 1 (2): 129–136.

➢ Baumeister, R. F.; Stillwell, A. M.; Heatherton, T. F. (1994). "Guilt: An interpersonal approach". Psychological Bulletin. 115 (2): 243–267. doi:10.1037/0033-2909.115.2.243. PMID 8165271.

➢ Clare, K. (2013). “How to Kill a Vampire: Crucifixes, Holy Water and Other Sacred Objects.” [Blog post. Retrieved from https://49thshelf.com/Blog/2013/10/31/How-to-Kill-a-Vampire-Crucifixes-Holy-Water-and-Other-Sacred-Objects]

➢ Evango, Patrick. “Why Do Vampires Hate Holy Water.” [Video File]. Retrieved from https://www.youtube.com/watch?v=EFBSL3gT9Kc

➢ Suzuki, A., Sakurazawa, H., Fujita, T., & Akamatsu, R. (2016). Overeating at dinner time among Japanese workers: Is overeating related to stress response and late dinner times? *Appetite,101*, 8-14. doi:10.1016/j.appet.2016.02.145

➢ Xu, H.; Bègue, L.; Bushman, B. J. (2012). "Too fatigued to care: Ego depletion, guilt, and prosocial behavior". Journal of Experimental Social Psychology. 43 (5): 379–384. doi:10.1016/j.jesp.2012.03.007.

➢ Wikipedia contributors. (2019, May 20). Ego depletion. In Wikipedia, The Free Encyclopedia. Retrieved 08:43, June 10, 2019, from https://en.wikipedia.org/w/index.php?title=Ego_depletion&oldid=898027551

Day Nine – Practical Steps

Step 1: Review Your Existing Self Care Routine

Review the list of self-care opportunities in the section above and take stock of which you are already doing, how often, and what impact you feel each has on you.

Step 2: Integrate More Self Care into Your Day By Defining NBA Self-Care Rules

Plan to integrate at least two additional self-care breaks for yourself during the day tomorrow. They can be as small as 5 minutes each, or as long as you have time to accommodate. Determine how you could do this on a regular basis.

Now define NBA rules that regulate your self-care.

Really!

Without rules, these ideas are just that, ideas!

In addition to the rules, figure out how you will remind yourself to implement them. This is particularly important for self-care rules. Will you set an alarm? Leave them as recurring tasks on your to-do list until they are completed each day? Write down and execute this plan, especially if Pigula says you shouldn't!

> "You've tried a million times to add self-care to your day and never succeeded, so why in the world do you think you can be successful this time? Muhahaha! Let's just skip the whole thing and buy a dozen donuts for tonight's pig party!" -Pigula

As usual, Pigula has a point, it's difficult to change your routine. This is because we are creatures of habit. In the same way we have "programmed" ourselves to overeat at night, we have also programmed ourselves to eat lunch and rush right back to work without any time to pause, reflect, refresh, and renew. Adding a 5 min break after lunch to talk to a friend or take a little time for ourselves seems difficult because we're likely to forget.

This is where James Clear's idea of habit-stacking *(from his book "Atomic Habits")* comes in.

Habit stacking is a technique that allows you to add your new habit to an existing activity that you are *already* always doing during the day. For example, let's say you want to listen to an audiobook, twice during the day for 5 minutes. In this case you might create a rule that says...

I never fill my coffee cup at work without listening to an audiobook for 5 minutes first!

The perfect way to build a habit stack is to stack your new, desired habit onto an existing, FUN activity. This way, the fun activity acts as a reward to your new activity and quickly programs your mind to want to perform the new one.

> "But you'll forget that too, you silly nilly"
>
> The Count of Transpigvenia

True, that might happen, but if you review your Never Binge Again plan daily and make a real effort to remember, soon you'll discover you DO remember your new self-care routine and it becomes more and more second nature to do it.

Day Ten – Enhancing Your Self Care

Day Ten – Practical Steps

Step 1: Review your new self-care routines

Review the impact the additional self-care breaks you installed into your day had on you yesterday, both in terms of your nighttime food cravings AND on your personal wellbeing. Take detailed notes. Take a breath and ask yourself how you might revise and enhance this plan today.

Step 2: Increase your adherence to the rules

- ➢ Create and install a reminder system to keep up the additional self-care tasks you added to your day. What will trigger the breaks? How will you remember? If you have a daily morning journaling habit, you may also wish to incorporate an evaluation of the impact it's had on you.

- ➢ Revisit another meal using the flavor enhancement principles from Day six. Alternatively, begin going through the recipes section of this book and flag two healthy ones you'd like to make in the upcoming week.

CHAPTER 10: WHAT IF YOU OVEREAT AT NIGHT DESPITE EARNESTLY AND PASSIONATELY EXECUTING THIS PROTOCOL?

The first time you make a mistake you'll almost certainly hear something like this from your Pigula:

> "You cheated! You cheated! You cheated!!! See? Your Food Plan doesn't mean anything at all! The Hell with this *'Kitchen is Closed!'* stuff. You'll have to try something else to control me. YOU'VE BLOWN IT SO I AM NOW TOTALLY FREE TO BINGE AT WILL FROM NOW ON!!! Muhahahahaha!!! Party Time!!! Let's Do It!!!!" – Count Pigula The First

This one Whisper causes more damage than virtually any other because it allows a small departure from your food plan to snowball into a full-blown nighttime food orgy which seriously undermines confidence in your ability to control yourself.

This Whisper is wholly responsible for the "Screw it, you already blew it, just start again tomorrow" mentality. Or, in shorthand, the "F___ It" Whisper.

Learning to recognize and ignore the F__ It Whisper is, without a doubt, the most significant benefit of the Never Binge Again approach.

Thankfully this Whisper, like every other, is easily defeated once you see it for what it is.

For example, we're sure you've heard the idea of "progress, not perfection" bandied about by the so-called experts. They may even quote scientific evidence which suggests perfectionism is a set up for bingeing and overeating.

While these are alluring ideas which can be helpful when placed in context, they unfortunately only tell HALF the story. What these half-truths fail to acknowledge is the significant difference in attitude required *before* vs. *after* a food mistake. Just like we can't walk on water or swim on dry land, we must maneuver very differently before vs. after a mistake. *(Remember, a mistake, for the sake of our discussion, is even one bite or swallow outside of your very well-defined Food Plan)*:

➢ **BEFORE A MISTAKE:** Your Food Plan is 100% perfect and final. You Will NEVER Make a Mistake Again. You Will NEVER Eat After The Kitchen is Closed Again!

➢ **AFTER A MISTAKE:** You are a fallible human being. You were *practicing* a set of Food Rules, but that practice is now over and it's time for the big leagues. Analyze what went wrong, adjust your Food Plan if necessary, and THEN declare it perfect and final. You may have found it necessary to divorce the old Food Plan *(or simply failed to hear Pigula's Whispers about it),* but now you're a changed person, ready to marry once again. You Will NEVER Party at night with Food Again!

Pigula wants to confuse these two situations so you'll reject your Food Plan as nonsensical. Why? So it can have its nightly food orgy!

I hope you're starting to see a pattern. Partying with food at night is ALL Pigula ever wants, and there's NEVER a reason to listen to it before, during, or after a mistake.

Pigula's "confuse and conquer" maneuver is easily defeated when you place your thinking in the right context.

WHY PERFECTION IS THE BEST COMMITMENT TOOL: Making a sacred commitment to your Food Plan is like getting married. And We've yet to hear these vows at a wedding ceremony:

> "I promise to love and be faithful...until an inevitable moment of weakness. I promise I'll do the best I can, but nobody's perfect and there sure are a lot of attractive people out there. I'm 80% sure I can be faithful forever, but anyone who promises you 100% is an unrealistic liar. A 'pretty good' promise is the best anyone can ever hope for, because you can't possibly know who you're going to sleep with next year, or in ten years. Just being honest. You want me to be honest, right?" – The

Vow Pigula Would Make at Its Wedding!

You'd never accept this kind of a wishy-washy promise from a mate...so why entertain it for your own commitments? Pigula craves uncertainty, not you. It will exploit even the most miniscule crisis of confidence to tear at the very fabric of your most sacred vows.

Time for another thought experiment: Suppose your fiancé—*after realizing you wouldn't accept this level of uncertainty in the wedding vows*—increased their confidence in a lifetime of fidelity from 80% to 90%. Would you marry them then?

What about 95%?

99%?

Kind of ruins the romance, doesn't it!

You wouldn't accept anything less than a 100% commitment, because perfection is the essence of commitment...all notions of human frailty aside.

PERFECTION IS ESSENCE OF COMMITMENT

Allowing ANY possibility you will ever Party with food again changes the commitment from "I will" to "I'll try" ...which is NO commitment at all. The "little engine that could" was in error. "I think I can" is the wrong philosophy. "I know I can" is the only attitude which succeeds with impulse control because Pigula will use "I'll try" to destroy the very fabric of your Food Plan.

Anything less than a plan for 100% adherence to your Food Plan is nothing more than Pigula's plan to party with food. You must authoritatively declare your Food Plan as 100% perfect or you are not committing to anything at all.

The philosophy behind "progress not perfection" as a *before* tool is one of hopeless abandon to Pigula's impulses. To adopt the "progress not perfection" ideology is to believe it's literally impossible to dominate your Cravings.

Progress-not-perfection says there will eventually come an irresistible urge which forces you to indulge, it's just a matter of time.

Cravings are indeed a natural part of being alive. You can't escape them, but once you've drawn your perfect lines in the sand you need not fear them either!

Now, there actually IS scientific evidence that perfectionism is a set up for overeating and bingeing, but what's missing from this analysis is context. Perfectionism is *only* a set up for a Binge when you allow Pigula to use it to retrospectively assign powerlessness to you—*AFTER* a mistake has occurred:

> "Either you're perfect or you're nothing. Either you can perfectly control your food intake or you can't control it at all. You made a mistake and are therefore not perfect. Obviously, you are now completely out of control. I get to go on a big giant hairy Binge. Yippeeee!!!" - Pigula

Perfectionism may be a set up for a downward spiral when you apply it after a mistake has occurred, but when you use it to lock in your commitments at the outset just the opposite is true. Perfectionism is the right approach to gain control of your eating forever when used as a commitment tool. In fact, in this context I'd contend it is the ONLY approach that works. However, when applied as a post-food-mistake analysis tool it works in Pigula's best interest, not yours.

To never overeat at night again and permanently stick to our commitments we must recognize any and all insecurity as 100% Pigula Whispers. By definition, it can't be any other way because a Pigula Whisper is any thought, feeling, or impulse which suggests you will *ever* overeat at night again for any reason whatsoever... from now until the day you die.

Any and all doubt about your commitment to your food plan is a Pigula Whisper.

Now, what if you DO overeat at night? Can you feel how excited Pigula is getting about the fact we're even bothering to write this?

> "See, these guys know we ARE going to party tonight, otherwise they'd never put this section in the book. I'm so happy!!! Let's go already. Let's just do it!!!! C'mon already!!!" – Pigula

What if you DO overeat at night? What then???

Simple: Analyze what happened, adjust your sails, and then NEVER overeat again.

Why? Because the Pigula must be nailed shut in its coffin, that's why!

Period, end of story.

Notwithstanding the simplicity and elegance of this instruction, many people feel the need for more direction to get back on track after a mistake. So, let's talk about the right mental maneuvers to recover from a mistake.

First, please know that after a mistake Pigula will direct all its efforts to *building* upon your mistake. And like all vampires,

Pigula is terrified of the light of day and prefers to hide in the dark. It knows under scrutiny you will become wise to its game, so it will try to get you to casually dismiss the mistake without examination—in hopes of keeping the errors in thinking and/or problematic Food Rules from being exposed.

In short, Pigula will martial all its efforts to stop you from carefully reflecting upon what happened and instead try to direct your energy towards eating MORE.

Knowing Pigula's post-mistake goals, the first thing to do after a mistake is remember what a serious, solemn oath committing to our Food Plan actually was. After all, your ability to stick with your own commitments is your ability to keep your word, and without your word, you don't have much. So, if you find you've made a mistake you must take it *very* seriously and become willing to carefully reflect upon what went wrong.

On the other hand, creating the perfect set of Food Rules for any given individual is a complex matter... not unlike creating a set of laws to govern a large, interactive society.

Successful legal systems always contain a mechanism for self-correction. For example, although the framers of the United States Constitution fully intended it to govern as the law of the land, they understood it was still a potentially fallible document. So, they included a mechanism for amending it over time.

But the process for amending the Constitution does *not* allow for impulsivity. It requires a drawn-out process of proposals, votes, and ratification. These delays ensure serious consideration is given to the ramifications of change and make it difficult for any one crazed person *(or group)* to seize power and undo all the good work.

Therefore, the first thing to do after a mistake is to examine what happened. Review your Food Plan with an eye towards determining whether you believe each Food Rule within it is still in your best interest.

Is the Food Plan as a whole still the most accurate representation of a perfect, healthy lifestyle? Or does something need to be amended?

More often than not, mistakes occur simply because you failed to hear the Pigula's Whisper, NOT because of a problem with the Food Plan itself. Pigula slipped in a few destructive words which you mistook for your own thinking, and you acted upon them.

This is called a "Simple Pigula Attack" and requires NO changes to your Plan. If you've experienced a Simple Pigula Attack just put Pigula back in its coffin forever by re-committing in full to the exact Food Plan you just broke.

But remember, Pigula will fight violently because it doesn't want to go back into its coffin, once again locked away from its Slop forever. Listen for things like:

> "You obviously can't lock me in my coffin forever. You're too weak. I just got out, so of course I'll get out again. Maybe I can't beat you now but it's only a matter of time until we party again. Muhahaha!!!"– Pigula's response upon hearing you will never party with food again after a recent indulgence

This is utter Pigula Whisper and has NO constructive purpose. Pigula doesn't care about your well-being at all. It ONLY wants Slop, so why would you ever take its thoughts seriously?

Just ignore Pigula on this matter, don't debate it.

Notwithstanding the above, having rational answers for this nonsense is helpful to many people as they're first learning how to put Pigula back in its coffin. So, let's address the Pigula's "points":

- "You're too weak" → Making a renewed effort to eat more constructively is evidence of strength, not weakness. Even if you've repeatedly fallen down for years, continuing to get up until you succeed is a mark of fortitude and perseverance, not weakness. A weak person just listens to Pigula and gives up. A strong one *(like Dr. Van Helsing in many vampire movies)* resolves to lock Pigula back in its coffin forever. Making a renewed vow proves your strength. When you think about it this way, you'll see how truly pathetic it is that Pigula would attempt to use your renewed vow against you!

- "I just got out, so of course I'll get out again." → It's extremely unusual for prisoners to break out of jail twice unless the jailor consciously and purposefully leaves the door open.

- "Maybe I can't beat you right now but it's only a matter of time until we party with food again." → Since you have full control over what you buy, open, take out of the package with your hands, put in your mouth, chew, and swallow, you will *always* have the 100% ability to keep Pigula in its coffin. You don't have to worry about "later", only the present, and it is always the present.

That's how to defeat Pigula after a simple Pigula Attack.

But what if you believe your Food Plan itself was at fault?

For example, what if YOU *(not Pigula!)* believe you've erroneously committed to a Plan which is too restrictive and leaves you uncomfortably hungry and/or missing key nutrients by the time the day comes to a close?

If this is the case you're going to need to go ahead and change it. But before you do (a) be sure you've given yourself some time for the Slop you've ingested to leave your system because it's hard to hear the Pigula's Whispers when your body's full of Slop; (b) Save a dated copy of your complete Food Plan before making any changes so you can roll it back later if you find Pigula has influenced the changes; (c) Take some serious, reflective time to "think on paper" about the specific changes you're planning to make; (d) Consider whether any previous version of your Food Plan was better. It's not unusual for mistakes to have occurred because Pigula convinced you to abandon a perfectly good Food Plan. If this is the case, just revert to the old one. And since you save a dated copy of every version, this is easy to do.

Here's one more thing to consider as you re-examine your Food Plan: If you find you're repeatedly struggling with a food or drink in the Conditionals section, the odds are pretty good you need to move it to the Nevers. For many people, certain super-rewarding foods taste and feel too good to constrain with conditions and rules. But these same people—*who may have struggled for years or even decades with a particular food*—find it remarkably easy to NEVER have it again. Certainly much easier than the ongoing, painful search for that one "magic rule" which will let them have their cake and eat it too.

Never can be a LOT easier than sometimes!

Last, during the "legislative process"—*the time during which you are re-examining your Food Plan*—it's best if you allow the previous rules to govern, however imperfect they may be. Pigula craves the anarchy which underlies an eating mistake. Therefore, under no circumstances should you ever allow "the absence of a government" to exist—even for a micro-second.

And remember, you made a mistake, you didn't have a brain operation which disabled your ability to make good food choices, or to control your hands, arms, legs, mouth, and tongue. You have not had a mysterious curse laid upon you which prevents you from eating well. Space aliens have not abducted you and implanted electrodes which force you to eat junk. Whatever new rules you may consider, you are 100% in charge of feeding yourself throughout the entire process! Finally...

After a serious analysis of what caused the mistake, promptly forgive yourself and make a 100% confident, renewed commitment to *perfectly* follow your Food Plan forever.

You are a fallible human being. You were *practicing* a particular Food Plan, but now practice is over. It's time for the big leagues. You analyzed what went wrong, and made the necessary adjustments so...

You Will Party with Food at Night Again!

Lock Pigula in its coffin and keep it there!

CHAPTER 11: JUST ONE BITE OFF YOUR FOOD PLAN IS AN INVITATION FOR THE VAMPIRE (PIGULA) TO ENTER YOUR HOME

We take a LOT of heat for defining a mistake as just one bite off your carefully constructed Food Plan. Some critics say it's an impossible standard and we're just setting people up to fail.

But we continue to insist our students refer to a single bite off their food plan as a mistake because of the following:

It defines a very clear target and prevents Pigula from blurring the lines around your food rules.

If we didn't refer to every bite outside of our food plan as a mistake, then would you be allowed to eat "just one piece" of chocolate at night despite having a "No chocolate after 7pm" rule? Would it be ok to eat a couple of pieces? How about six pieces if you had a small lunch? If the line is NOT really a line, then where IS the line? *(Hint: There is none!)*

You see, it's much easier for Pigula to whisper in your ear and get you to break your rules if they are fuzzy.

Having a rock solid, unbreakable plan allows you to immediately recognize any and all Pigula Whispers and summarily ignore them.

In contrast, with a fuzzy plan, you're leaving the door wide open for Pigula to come in. That creature only needs a little slit left open to barrel in at full speed. You can be damn sure it'll squeeze through any opening to wreak havoc!

REMEMBER: Every time you cave into the urge, Pigula grows stronger. Yes, it really IS that simple. Reward the urge to eat at night and you strengthen the nighttime eating habit. Even if it's "just one bite." As noted previously, we are creatures of habit. Reward the urge and strengthen the habit, resist the urge and you weaken it!

That said, you also do NOT have to eat the entire contents of the fridge if you find yourself having made a mistake. See, one of Pigula's favorite whispers is "You blew it! You ate one cookie/piece of chocolate/whatever and now your ENTIRE plan is worthless. So why not have a full-on food orgy. Like in the good ole' days!"

Please read the following carefully because understanding and implementing the following idea can (and likely WILL) dramatically change your life...

Rebounding quickly and learning from mistakes is the key to successfully stopping the nighttime eating habit...and indeed, to almost anything else in life.

If instead of listening to Pigula, you say to yourself...

"Oops, I made a mistake, that's not good, but not the end of the world. First off, I'm going to resume my eating plan right away! Then I'm going to figure out why I made the mistake and if needed, change my Food Rules/diet to avoid doing it again" ...

Then you are heading quite rapidly towards success.

On the other hand, listening to Pigula's "You blew it, so you might as well screw it" Whisper is a sure-fire way to lose the game.

Mistakes are unavoidable. If you demonize them, you give them power.

Now here's the rub...

Even if we did NOT define even one single bite off your Food Plan or diet as a binge, you'd still eventually make a mistake that YOU would characterize as a binge.

If you approach every mistake with a mindset which assumes you can't learn and improve—which is what happens when you fail to discern small misses as binges—then that mistake becomes a failure. And once you've failed, you've failed!

Pigula would love for you to adopt this fixed-failure mindset because then, when the next mistake happens, you will abandon your plan altogether, and it will once again rule your nights until the day you die. In other words, the "little mistakes don't count" mindset actually ensures Pigula will win.

However, if you approach your mistakes with a growth mindset *—one which assumes you can and will learn and improve with EVERY mistake*—then you start seeing mistakes as opportunities. Every mistake is a chance to make better Food Rules, as well as to more clearly identify and recognize Pigula's Whispers.

Pigula is deadly afraid of the growth mindset, because it is a no-nonsense practical approach which ruthlessly shines light on Pigula's Squeals and eliminates every loophole in your Food Plan.

Plus... with a growth mindset, mistakes are NO LONGER a source of agonizing shame and regret. You may experience SOME regret and shame right after the mistake, but only enough to energize you to solve the problem. Once you've taken the necessary steps to solve the problem, the shame and regret disappear. After all, it's only common sense. After accidentally a hot stove, one only needs to feel pain long enough to notice where the stove was so they can avoid doing it again. There's no point to saying "OMG, I'm a pathetic hot stove toucher, I might as well put my whole hand down on the grill!"

The growth mindset is a much gentler, better way to live, and we warmly suggest you adopt it! *(With everything you do – not just your eating).*

CHAPTER 12: PIGULA'S DEPRIVATION TRAP

> *"You simply can't quit the nighttime food parties! You'll feel way too deprived and eventually you'll just give up and feed me. Why wait? Let's Do It Now!!!" – Sincerely, Pigula*

> "There, there now. You're very upset. Go get us some comfort food and let's have ourselves a little party. We'll feel SOOOOO much better! And we'll start this 'diet' thing tomorrow." – Sincerely, Pigula

There are actually TWO types of deprivation: (1) What you deprive yourself of by NOT having something and; (2) what you deprive yourself of by having it. *(To our knowledge, this was first pointed out by Geneen Roth)*

It's exceptionally rare for people to consciously choose between these two alternatives. In fact, most people never consider the second kind at all.

Just for illustration—*I'm NOT saying you have to adopt this rule*—let's take the notion of never eating ice-cream at night again. If you decide to never eat ice-cream at night again, you'll deprive yourself of the taste, texture, and mouth feel of ice-cream while watching late-night TV, for the rest of your natural life. You will never experience TV-Watching-Ice-Cream-Pleasure again. To the ice-cream-loving Pigula, this is most certainly a fate worse than death.

But if you decide to *continue* eating ice-cream while watching TV, you will deprive yourself of everything associated with *never* mindlessly eating ice-cream again including (a) acquiring the body of your dreams *(or something very close); (b) The deep and healing sleep which never comes when you are bloated and full of sugar (c) waking up feeling healthy and energetic and not bloated and tired (d)* the "lightness of being" associated with life without all that extra weight; (d) the energy associated with more regular, healthy nourishment; (e) knowing what it's like to have consistent blood sugar levels and to live without sugar crashes; (f) the *confidence* which comes from knowing you have the power to control yourself around food; (g) years near the end of your life which were meant to be pain-free and full of joy, but are instead filled with immobility and dysfunction due to strokes, heart attacks, etc.

Pigula would love to have you concentrate only on the *short-term* effects of deprivation because it genuinely believes its Slop is the *only* pleasure life has to offer. But the list of things we deprive ourselves of by *continuing* a food behavior is often a lot longer, and much more painful!

To take advantage of this insight you only need to make a solid comparison between your two choices. What will you deprive yourself of if you continue to embrace a particular food *(or food behavior)* in the evening?

And I'll tell you what, let's give Pigula a running start by letting it go first. Think about your sundown demarcation line, and how you're going to clap your hands, say "Kitchen is Closed" and stop eating until morning. Now, go ahead and tell Pigula to provide you with a long list of things you'll be depriving yourself of if you never eat this particular food at night again.

Can you feel Pigula squirming? That's because there are only two things it can really put forward in this situation—taste and convenience. Oh, it will say you'll be depriving yourself of life itself—that you'll starve to death in a matter of hours without its favorite Slop.

But by now Pigula knows you're on to that game. So, the best it can do is say "because it tastes good" or "it's going to be too complicated to eat well throughout the day."

Pigula squirms at the mere thought of this exercise because it knows its ammunition pales in comparison to your side of the equation.

Send Pigula to its coffin...write down your list!

Let Pigula say as much as it wants about how deprived you'll feel when you close the kitchen at the hour YOU deem is best...

When you write these things down it should become clear to you Pigula is talking about itself. It will feel deprived, not you.

Then write down everything you can think of which YOU will be deprived of by heeding Pigula's advice and 'keeping the kitchen open'.

A well-considered, informed decision between the two types of deprivation always favors YOU, so just write down the facts and make your choices.

One last important point about all this...

You make the rules. So be sure you've created a Food Plan you're confident you can live with forever. One which allows you to pursue your dreams in the body you want, while striking the optimal balance between short term pleasures vs. longer term goals. Every rule you make is a compromise between these two ends. Only you can decide where the best line is for your own body—that's what freedom is about!

Here's another way to look at it: Every day we make choices between "Live Fast and Die Young[1]" vs. "Live Slow and Enjoy the Long Ride." Do you want to borrow life from tomorrow to live faster today, or forgo some short-term pleasure to achieve a better long-term outcome?

In a free country, we have every right to trade suffering tomorrow for pleasure today if this is what we truly desire. In fact, we've fought wars for this kind of freedom.

However, the problem is most people have allowed Pigula to dominate these decisions, so they never make a conscious choice. And because they've never experienced long periods of Pigula-free eating, they also haven't had the opportunity to make informed decisions about these very critical food matters.

I might not agree, but I'd vehemently defend your right to say "I'm choosing to live a little faster right now for the sheer pleasure of it. I'm fully aware I'm probably going to die a little younger and/or suffer more at the end of my life because of this choice, but I'm of sound mind, adult years, and 100% capable of making this conscious choice."

The problem is, people making this tradeoff rarely do so consciously. Instead, they allow Pigula to pull the wool over their eyes and keep them blind to these choices.

The ultimate responsibility of freedom is choosing whether to live fast and die young vs. enjoy the longer, slower ride. However you may decide on any particular Food Rule, please be sure you've given yourself a chance to experience the slower side of the equation so you're making a truly informed choice.

CHAPTER 13: PIGULA IS POWERLESS, NOT YOU

Let's conduct a little experiment, shall we?

We'd like you to hold your right hand up so that you can see the palm of your hand.

Now, tell Pigula the following...

"Pigula, please move my pinky!"

Don't move it yourself, just tell Pigula to move your pinky and wait.

Did it move?

Of course not!

Now, please tell Pigula the following...

"Pigula, if you move my little finger now, I'll buy you whatever you want to eat, and we'll gobble it up together tonight!"

Don't cheat, don't move the finger yourself. Hold it in place and wait for Pigula to move it.

Did Pigula succeed?

Well... we both know it didn't.

You see, you are the only one in control of your body. Only you can get up, walk to the fridge, take out the boxes and containers, open them and then move your hands to feed yourself.

The only thing that Pigula can do is create an URGE to eat within you.

But it is up to YOU to act on the urge. Pigula can't do that!

Contrary to the popular opinion in the addiction industry, we believe you are not sick. That you have not contracted a 'food addiction disease'. We believe so simply because, until someone shows us evidence to the contrary, we've seen no compelling scientific data to support the existence of such a wildly hypothetical disease. Nobody has identified a common over-eating virus or germ. Except for serious brain damage, there are no malfunctioning organs found responsible for overeating. And although you *could* say overeating occurs because of a malfunction in the brain, it is our opinion the simpler explanation is correct, nighttime eating is merely a strong habit, reinforced daily with powerful rewards.

The fact the rewards are so pleasurable *(sugar, salt, fat, etc.)* and that the habit was reinforced repeatedly *(daily, in most cases)* for years, makes it more difficult to break, but that's just the way humans are wired. We strive to continue doing that which makes us feel better. It doesn't mean we have a night-time eating disease that can't be cured. Overeating at night is a nasty habit, but it can be broken by simply withholding the reward long enough. If you don't overeat at night the urge MUST eventually subside dramatically because there'll no longer be any biological sense for it to continue.

The bottom line is, Pigula hasn't infected you with a chronic, incurable nighttime eating disease. All it can do is create a physical urge within you. When you resist the urge and instead choose to take authentic care of yourself, it will talk your ear off in an attempt to convince you to move your body and get its Slop...

Until it eventually learns there's NO point in (and NO reward for) this effort.

Pigula is a weak, single-minded creature which doesn't care about anything besides gorging. It will extract any price from your life to get at its Slop, but it's completely powerless to do so unless you listen to its Whispers.

Pigula is powerless and you are its master.

So, just turn a deaf ear and just never overeat at night again!

Note: We're legally required to inform you that notwithstanding what's said in this chapter there are some serious eating disorders —including but not limited to bulimia, anorexia, and binge eating disorder—which do require professional assistance. Only a licensed professional can diagnose and treat eating disorders)

Last Note: We got the idea for the "wiggle your pinky" technique from Jack Trimpey at Rational Recovery, who uses something very similar to help people who struggle with drugs and alcohol to reassure themselves they have the power to stop.

CHAPTER 14: HOW TO STOP FEELING SHAME AND GUILT ABOUT YOUR EATING MISTAKES (A RADICAL WAY TO USE GUILT AND SHAME IN YOUR LIFE)

Can you use shame, guilt and regret to better yourself?

It's an odd notion isn't it?

But, as usual, we're going to present you with a radically different approach.

See, while the vast majority of the mental health community suggests you focus on loving yourself and accepting yourself completely *(including your bad habits)* in order to rid yourself of shame and guilt, we propose something completely different: We propose you consider using shame, guilt and regret in a very active way against Pigula!

You execute this plan somewhat differently before vs. after you've committed to a solving your nighttime overeating problem. Let's begin with the time *before* you resolved to solve your nighttime eating problem and created a concrete plan to do so. Before this commitment is made in earnest everyone's favorite method (including Pigula's) is to attempt a complete suppression of the inevitable feelings of shame and regret which accompany serious food mistakes. It seems we are so very afraid of these feelings; we'll do anything and everything we can to distract ourselves from them:

- We bury ourselves in work...
- Or by caring for others *(even if they really don't need that much help)* ...
- We numb ourselves by watching mindless entertainment on TV or Netflix...
- We hypnotize ourselves by scrolling endlessly through Facebook, Instagram or the latest social network...
- And let's not forget the best distraction of them all... Pigula's favorite... we Party with food!

Unfortunately, as you most likely already know, suppression only makes you feel better for a little while. In the long run it makes the problem worse because the distracting behaviors lead to even more overeating *(and low-value behaviors),* which only produce *more* shame, guilt and regret...and the cycle continues!

Therefore, instead of distracting yourself from the uncomfortable feelings which accompany an eating mistake, we suggest putting them to use! You may be surprised to learn there's no reason to be deadly afraid of shame, guilt, and regret since, in the right doses, they are intended to serve a natural, healthy function in human psychology. Shame, guilt, and regret exist to draw your attention to something which requires fixing. They're your mind's way of signaling you that something needs to change so you can avoid repeating negative results. Shame, guilt, and regret are kind of like the sharp-but-short-lived pain you feel when you touch a hot stove to help ensure you don't do it again.

You're supposed to FEEL these feelings intensely enough to get your attention and ensure you make the necessary adjustments, but they're not supposed to get "stuck" inside you. Once you've made the adjustments *(e.g. after examining your plans and committing 100% to never touching that hot stove again)* you're supposed to let them go.

Remember: You are definitely NOT the only person in the world with a nighttime overeating problem. In fact, 57% of the US population shares this difficulty. So as awful as you may feel, and as much as Pigula may be trying to make you feel like the worst person in the world *(so you'll feel too weak to resist its next nighttime overeating impulse),* there are tens of millions of people suffering in exactly the same way you are, having made very similar mistakes at any given moment. You might be interested to know that BOTH myself (Glenn) and Yoav had serious eating problems. VERY serious!

So, instead of being deadly afraid of these feelings, consider exploring them a little bit. It may feel painful to articulate them in black and white, but once it's done, you'll discover a new kind of energy. An ANGER towards Pigula for trying to make you feel so awful which will strengthen your resolve tenfold.

We therefore suggest you brace yourself and write down the list of things which you feel ashamed of regarding your food and weight problems. To get you started, I asked Yoav if he'd share some things he was ashamed of when he started his weight loss journey. Here's the list he came up with:

- I am VERY ashamed of the way I look
- I feel completely unattractive
- I feel disgusting
- I feel like everyone around me treats me like less of a person *(and less of a man)* because I am so overweight
- I feel weak and pathetic
- I'm afraid my wife will eventually lose interest in me because of the way I look

Harsh stuff, isn't it? But you can either suppress such feelings by freeing Pigula and letting it numb you with sugar, salt, and fat. Or you can become hot steaming mad at Pigula for bringing you to this point in your life.

Yoav did the latter. After experiencing the pain of realizing he how ashamed and displeased he was with himself, he vowed to never let himself be in this position again. That commitment provided tremendous energy which he used to lose 90 pounds. Yoav is now slim, athletic and proud!

Important Note: We are not suggesting this is an easy process. In fact, from our own experience, as well as that of the hundreds of clients we've helped come to terms with how they feel about the damage they've caused themselves by listening to Pigula for years, we know it can be difficult. But it can also be extremely rewarding if you approach it with a growth mindset. Just acknowledge where you truly are now and resolve to become better. Plus, remember the intensity of these feelings is almost always purposefully exaggerated by Pigula to weaken you and make you feel more open to listening to its nighttime Whispers.

(Once most people realize the intensity of the shame and guilt is coming from Pigula's binge-motivated efforts it becomes a lot easier to let those feelings go.)

Another important note: If you feel going through this process on your own will be too difficult, we suggest finding a licensed mental health professional to help. Regardless, please remember you do not want to repress your feelings and accept your bad habits, you want to experience the pain and understand what's been going on all these years so you can truly 100% resolve to make yourself better.

Also, there's NO need to constantly focus on feelings of shame and guilt about food mistakes. Once you've made a concrete plan to use these powerful emotions to change your situation for the better, just let go and just focus on the NEW, healthy behaviors you want to implement in your life.

Once you're on your way to implementing the system described in this book, once you've seen how to leverage these harsh emotions for your own benefit, you'll want to become MUCH kinder to yourself when you make mistakes. In the end, what you want to do is step OFF the emotional shame rollercoaster which has been helping Pigula rob you of the mental energy required to ignore it. You'll want to let go of these feelings, just let them pass through you quickly, and move on.

As a practical matter if you make a mistake after you've defined your plan and committed to follow it, then use the brief-but-sharp pain of shame, guilt, and regret as a little signal which suggests you pay closer attention. Maybe the purpose of this signal is to point out your Food Plan has a hole in it which requires fixing. Perhaps you need to amend one of your rules to stop Pigula from deceiving you in the future. Or maybe you were just absent minded and followed one of Pigula's Whispers as if it were your own thought, in which case you should simply resolve to be more vigilant in the future.

Don't let Pigula talk you into fearing your guilt...

Or holding onto it once you've fixed the problem.

Food mistakes do burn indeed ...

But if you're a human being who's still breathing, you've got a miraculously strong ability to recover and leave that mistake in the past.

Lock Pigula in its coffin and watch how fast it loses power! "Commit with perfection but forgive yourself with dignity."

One final thought... we know this is a very different way to think about shame and guilt, but hey, your mind is yours to control. You can choose to use your emotions as you please. So instead of being a slave to them, you can choose to use them to your benefit. After all, it's your mind!

CHAPTER 15: YOUR PERSONAL PIGULA WHISPERS JOURNAL

As we've discussed to this point, all that's necessary to partying with food at night is to define a Demarcation Line, make sure you get adequate sustenance throughout the day, and optionally add a few regular self-care activities.

This can be fully done by defining a Food Plan, committing to it with a 100% certain resolution, and then going about the rest of your life.

All you need to do is comply with your Food Plan, and utterly ignore any thought *(Pigula Whisper)* which suggests you do otherwise.

Journaling is therefore NOT a requirement of the program.

That said, you can only ignore a Pigula Whisper if you recognize it. And—*especially in the beginning*—Pigula will be busy dreaming up NEW ways to disguise its Whispers. After all, Pigula doesn't want to be locked in a coffin forever. It will passionately work to find loopholes.

Ultimately all Pigula's reasons boil down to "because it tastes good" or "because I want the Food High" ...and it will eventually stop bothering you when it realizes you know this. Like all wild animals in captivity it realizes there's no use continuing to bang on the inside of a permanently locked door.

But because Pigula lives inside you and has access to your native thinking, every person will hear different types of Whispers during the adjustment phase, so it's impossible to list every last possibility in this book.

For this reason, journaling can be very helpful.

Journaling sensitizes you to how Pigula sounds when it attempts a new Whisper. Wait, what's that? We can hear Pigula now:

> "These guys are saying you've got to journal or else you won't hear my super-creative NEW reasons for partying with food at night. This means the first day you forget and/or don't have the time to journal we can go off to the races and Binge our little faces off. Muhahahaha!!!"

Pigula Whisper!

You've unambiguously defined a Food Plan which draws clear lines in the sand...

You've solemnly sworn an oath to hold to it forever...

You CAN do this regardless of whether you journal or not.

But journaling makes it less stressful because you'll recognize the Whispers sooner. That's all.

Anyway, a simple way to go about this is to challenge Pigula each morning before you've eaten anything. Say "Go ahead Pigula. I'll give you control over my fingers to type/write any reason you can think of to convince me to feed you some Slop. Let's see if you can come up with a good one!"

It's OK. They're your fingers and you can take back control

whenever you like. And because you will NEVER overeat at night again, no matter what Pigula says, you can let Pigula have at it.

Once the Whispers are in black and white it takes less energy to recognize and ignore them.

Now, you'd think Pigula would catch on to this game and just stop playing after it realizes you're only baiting it to reveal its hand. But Pigula is so impulse driven it can't help but lunge at the opportunity. Again and again, no matter what the results were last time, the time before that, or the forty-two million times before *that!*

It's kind of like dangling roast beef in front of a Doberman Pincher. The chance to get the meat, however slim, is too alluring. Its primitive instincts will take over, no matter what happened before.

Just like the Doberman, Pigula will always give you its best shot if you dangle a nighttime food-party opportunity in front of it.

Stupid Pigula.

Back to the coffin with you!

CHAPTER 16: WHAT TO DO WHEN IT'S NOT WORKING

"What if it doesn't work?"

This question *itself* is a Pigula Whisper.

By definition, the Food Rules approach isolates and starves any and all overeating impulses so you can once again exercise free will with food. How you use that innate human capacity is entirely up to you.

If you choose to deploy free will to work for you, it WILL work for you. You literally can't fail, because all you're doing is letting go of an illusion and stepping squarely into the way things are.

If you choose to consciously and purposefully let Pigula out of its coffin, now that you know it's game, well, that's up to you too...

See, this program is about restoring your sense of free will and power. It's a fiercely independent philosophy...

You definitely CAN lock up Pigula forever – but you're the ONLY one who can.

If it works for you, we won't take credit...

But if it doesn't work, we won't take the blame either...

Because all we've really done is point out that YOU were in control all along.

We gave you permission to make your own Food Plan—*as if you really needed that from us?*—and a way to more clearly hear Pigula Whispering in your ear...

But the truth is, you were in Kansas all along, Dorothy!

We really do hope we've opened your eyes and empowered you...

And most importantly, we hope you now realize Pigula is NOT You!!!

APPENDIX A - DELICIOUS RECIPES MADE ENTIRELY FROM WHOLE FOODS

All of the following recipes are intended to help you enhance your food enjoyment with whole foods. To appeal to the largest possible variety of dietary philosophies each recipe includes a minimum of processed and/or industrial food, often is presented in both low (or modest) carbohydrate and high carbohydrate forms and may often be enhanced by adding lean plant and/or animal protein sources. In short, you should be able to adapt these recipes to increase the palatability and satisfaction of your overall diet no matter what your dietary philosophy may be!

Take the time to learn, make, and enjoy these recipes – you'll thank us, I promise.

Snacks/Sides/Small Dishes

Creamy Garlic Dill Sauce/Dip

Ingredients:

2 medium zucchinis, peeled and roughly chopped

1 handful of almonds (1/4 - 1/3 cup)*

juice of 1 lemon

a tiny sliver of onion *(We used yellow onion, but any will do. You can also use green onion for a milder flavor)*

1/4 - 1/2 c of fresh dill, to taste

garlic powder, to taste

Directions: Place all ingredients except the dill into the blender and blend until smooth. Add the dill and blend on medium low until it's chopped into tiny pieces. Use as a dressing, sauce, or even a dip!

*If you prefer a smoother dressing/sauce, you can use cashews instead of almonds.

Zucchini Fries

2 medium zucchinis, cut into fry sized shapes (you can peel or not, up to you)

½ c almond milk

½ c almond flour

¼ -1/2 tsp garlic powder

¼ – ½ tsp onion powder

Directions: Preheat oven to 350 degrees and line a baking sheet with parchment paper. Mix together almond flour, onion powder, and garlic powder in a bowl. Pour almond milk into a separate bowl. Dip each fry into the almond milk, then drop into the almond flour mixture and toss to coat, then place onto the baking sheet in a single layer. Repeat this process until all of your zucchini fries are coated. Bake 15 minutes, flip and bake another 15-20 minutes or until golden. The time may need to be adjusted up or down based on the size of your fries, so check on them every few minutes.

Mango Salsa

Ingredients:

2 large mangoes, diced

1/2 cucumber, diced

1/2 - 1 red, yellow, or orange bell pepper, diced

a sliver of red onion, or more to taste, minced (optional)

1/4 c cilantro, roughly chopped

lime juice, to taste

Jalapeno, to taste, minced (optional)

optional spices, to taste - cumin, paprika, chili powder, cayenne

Directions: Mix everything together and enjoy. I like to eat this as is, with a spoon or with lettuce leaves for dipping. You can also make it into wraps or eat it with chips or crackers.

Cauliflower Cilantro Rice

Ingredients:

½ medium onion, diced

oil for sautéing, optional

1 head cauliflower

1 stalk of green onion, finely chopped

¼ – ½ c cilantro, roughly chopped

1 lime

¼ c coconut milk *(optional for a creamier version)*

Directions: Pulse cauliflower in a food processor to a rice like size/consistency. Sauté the onion in a skillet on medium heat in a little water or 1 tsp oil until translucent. Add cauliflower to skillet and sauté, stirring occasionally to prevent sticking until cooked – about 5-10 minutes. If it becomes dry, add in water a little at a time to keep it moist and prevent it from sticking. At this point, add in the coconut milk, if using, as well as the green onion and cilantro. And cook for another 1-3 minutes.

Sweet Potato Hummus

Ingredients:

2 medium sweet potatoes, diced and boiled until completely soft (retain cooking water)

1/3 c tahini

¼ – ½ c lemon juice

1-2 garlic cloves

salt, to taste

cumin, to taste

Directions: Blend all ingredients until smooth. If necessary, add a little of the cooking water from the sweet potatoes to get the blades moving. *(More if you prefer a thinner consistency.)*

Entrees

Potato slices with Easy Homemade Marinara

Ingredients:

2 medium cooked sweet potatoes, sliced and baked or steamed

1 yellow onion, diced

3 cloves garlic, minced

½ c tomato paste

7-8 Roma tomatoes, depending on size, diced

Fresh basil, rosemary, and thyme to taste

Directions: sauté the onion and garlic in a little water or oil over medium heat until translucent. Add in the tomato paste and stir constantly for about 1 minute. Now add in the tomatoes and herbs. Bring to a simmer and reduce heat to medium low. Allow to simmer for 15-20 minutes or until desired flavor is developed. The longer it cooks, the thicker and more flavorful it will become. The sauce can be eaten as is, blended in a blender, or blended in the pot with an immersion blender. Use as a dipping sauce for your sweet potatoes.

Overstuffed Sweet Potato

Ingredients:

1 or 2 baked sweet potatoes, depending on size

½ onion, diced

1 c mushrooms, sliced

1 red, yellow, or orange bell pepper, diced

½ avocado, sliced

2 tbsp almond butter

2 tbsp lime juice

¼ c cilantro, roughly chopped

Chili powder, to taste

Directions: Sauté the onion and garlic on medium heat in a little water for about 3 minutes. Season with chili powder. Add the mushrooms and pepper and cook until done, stirring occasionally. Adjust seasoning as needed. Cut a slit into each sweet potato and top with the veggie mixture, avocado, and cilantro. For the almond butter sauce, simply whisk almond butter, lime, and water as needed to reach desired consistency. Pour over the sweet potatoes.

Taco Salad

Ingredients:

3 c romaine lettuce, thinly sliced

1 c black or pinto beans, either canned or precooked

1 medium tomato, diced

1 c salsa

1/2 c guacamole, see recipe below

1 ear of corn, cut off the cob

2 tbsp plain plant-based yogurt

10 olives

cilantro to taste, roughly chopped

lime juice, to taste

chili powder, to taste

Directions: Divide all the ingredients into serving bowls – creating 2-4 servings. Finish off with cilantro, chili powder, and lime juice.

Guacamole

Ingredients:

2 avocados

juice of 1-2 limes

¼ c cilantro, roughly chopped

salt, to taste

Directions: Mash the avocados with a fork to desired texture. Mix in the rest of ingredients. Adjust lime juice and salt to taste if necessary.

Asian Inspired Veggie Bowl

Ingredients

Veggies:

1 zucchini, peeled and julienned

2 large carrots, julienned

½ c purple cabbage, thinly sliced

½ red, yellow, or orange bell pepper, thinly sliced

1 c mung bean sprouts

Sauce:

1 ½ c mango (1-2 depending on size)

½ red, yellow, or orange bell pepper, roughly chopped

2 tbsp almond butter

1 tbsp lime juice

½ tsp fresh ginger

Directions: Place all of the veggies in a bowl. Blend all of the sauce ingredients except the ginger until smooth. Add the ginger and blend to incorporate. *(If ginger blends too long it becomes too strong and overpowering)* Pour the sauce over the veggies and toss to coat.

Quick Thai Coconut Curry

Ingredients:

A splash of oil or water for sautéing

½ medium onion, diced

3 garlic cloves, minced

½ tsp grated ginger

2 carrots, peeled and sliced into rounds

1 red, yellow, or orange bell pepper, thinly sliced

1 c mushrooms, thinly sliced

1 zucchini, cut into 1" long strips

1 can of coconut milk

juice of 1-2 limes

2-3 kaffir lime leaves, optional

1/3 c cilantro, roughly chopped

¼ c green onion, thinly sliced

Directions: Sauté onion and garlic in oil or water on medium heat in a pot or large saucepan, stirring often. Once the onion is translucent (about 3 minutes), add in the ginger, carrots, and bell pepper. Add water as needed to keep from drying out. Cover and allow to cook for 5-10 minutes. Now add in the zucchini, coconut milk, lime juice, lime leaves, cilantro, and green onion.

Cover again and allow to simmer until all vegetables are cooked to desired softness.

Pomegranate Rice Salad

Ingredients:

2 c cooked short grain brown rice

½ c green peas (either frozen and thawed or precooked)

½ c pomegranate

2 stalks celery, diced

1/3 c cilantro, roughly chopped

¼ c green onion, thinly sliced

¼ c raisins

juice of 1 lemon

Chinese 5 spice powder, to taste

cumin powder, to taste

coriander powder, to taste

½ avocado, diced, optional

Directions: Mix together all ingredients until well combined. Add in avocado, and gently mix again.

Butternut Mac and "Cheese"

Ingredients:

1 package of pasta of choice

1 onion, diced

3 cloves garlic, minced

Juice of 2 lemons

1 red bell pepper, roasted

2 c baked butternut squash

Vegetable broth

½ c cashews

Directions: If you are roasting your own bell pepper, place it on a baking dish in the oven on broil and cook until blackened on all sides. You'll have to turn it a few times. Cook pasta according to package instructions. While the pasta is cooking, saute the onion and garlic in a little water until translucent. When the pepper is done, allow to cool completely and then peel. Blend together all ingredients except for pasta adding enough vegetable broth to reach desired consistency. Pour over pasta and toss to coat.

Desserts/Sweet Things

Banana Ice Cream

Ingredients:

3 or more bananas, frozen ahead of time*

Directions: If using a high powdered blender, blend the bananas until smooth. If using a different blender, you may need to break the bananas up into small pieces and add a little water at a time. Only enough to get the blades moving. Blend until smooth.

Variation: Add other frozen fruits like mango, blueberries, and/or strawberries. You can also add a few spoonfuls of carob and/or cocoa powder for a chocolatey variation.

*it's best to peel the bananas before freezing.

Chocolate Milkshake

Ingredients:

2 or more frozen bananas

Almond or other plant-based milk

Cocoa or carob powder

Directions: Blend all ingredients in a blender until smooth. You can use as much or as little of the milk as you'd like depending on how thick you like your "milkshake". Same with the cocoa or carob powder. Add more for a richer, dark chocolate flavor, or less for a lighter flavor.

Sweet Peanut Butter Bites

Ingredients:

1 c rolled oats

½ c pecans

1/3 c peanut butter or peanut butter powder

1 ½ c dates, pitted

Directions: In a high-speed blender or food processor, blend the oats, pecans, and peanut butter or powder until crumbly. On high, add in dates a few at a time and blend until the mixture starts to hold together. Form into balls of desired size and enjoy!

Granola

Ingredients:

2 c oats

2/3 c almonds, whole or sliced, according to preference

2/3 c almond flour

¼ c chia seeds

½ c maple syrup

¼ tsp vanilla extract

Directions: Preheat oven to 325 degrees. Line a baking pan with parchment paper. You will either need 2 small pans or 1 large pan for this amount. Mix everything together and lay the mixture out on the pan in an even layer. Use a spoon or spatula to create some space here and there so that it's not one solid piece. Bake for 20 minutes. Mix granola with a spatula and bake another 5-15 minutes (peaking in every few minutes) or until golden. You'll know it's done when it starts to smell a little toasty. Allow to cool.

Notes:

- It won't be crunchy right when you take it out of the oven but will be once it cools.
- If you want to add dried fruit, do so after baking

Brownie Bites

Ingredients:

1 c rolled oats

1/2 c pecans

1/3 c carob or cocoa powder

1 1/2 c dates, pitted

Directions: In a high-speed blender or food processor, blend the oats, pecans, and carob until crumbly. On high, add in dates a few at a time and blend until the mixture starts to hold together. Form into balls of desired size and enjoy!

Strawberries with Chocolate Sauce

Ingredients:

1 pint strawberries, or however many you'd like

1 c dates, pitted

½ banana

¼ c cocoa or carob powder

Water or almond milk to reach desired consistency

Directions: Blend all ingredients except for the strawberries in a blender until smooth using enough liquid to reach the consistency you desire. Use as a dip for your strawberries or other fruit or add more water for a thinner version to use as a sauce for banana ice cream. You can even add hot water to create "hot fudge" for a hot fudge sundae with your banana ice cream.

Stuffed Dates with Coconut

Ingredients:

Equal number of medjool dates and pecan or halves

½ c shredded coconut

Directions: Cut a lengthwise slit in each date. Stuff each date with pecan half and roll in coconut.

APPENDIX B – MORE ABOUT VAMPIRE MYTHOLOGY

In the spirit of more thoroughly understanding the vampire metaphor utilized throughout this book we'd like to educate you more about vampiric legend. This is totally optional and not at all required to execute the ten-day protocol effectively.

The Vampire Slayer

NOTE: This is for illustration only and is used herein as a metaphor which can help you end nighttime overeating. We are only reporting on legend, and specifically recommend AGAINST trying to become a REAL vampire slayer, staking anyone or anything through the heart, and/or doing physical, emotional, and/or spiritual harm to any other person and/or animal, living, dead, and/or "undead."

The origin of the slayer legend, that is, the tale of a "chosen one" possessing mystical gifts for killing vampires, begins in the Eleventh Century, at a time when European Christians were expected to make annual pilgrimages to Jerusalem to visit the birthplace of their religion.

In 1050, Jerusalem reportedly was plagued by a major vampire outbreak. A papal army is reported to have driven the vampires into the hills surrounding the city, where the creatures of the night preyed upon pilgrims. There were reports that hundreds, perhaps thousands, of pilgrims lost their lives.

The legend says that, in response, Pope Urban II formed the Order of the Slayer in 1093. The pope asked wealthy warlords from Christian nations to assemble armies to march on Jerusalem to kill the predatory vampires. After they received specialized training, the Lords were welcomed into the Order in a solemn religious ceremony.

The Order filled its armies with volunteers who were given land in return for their service. The subsequent military campaign, known as the First Vampire Crusade, was a modest success. Each new outbreak in and around the Holy City prompted another Crusade, and the battle reportedly went on for nearly 300 years.

After the Crusades were over, the slayer lineage continued in the form of medieval Slayer Guilds, organizations of men trained in the art of fighting vampires. Since this trade, like any other of that time, was passed on from father to son, a population grew of warriors inherently possessing vampire-fighting capability. This notion continues today in the fringe community which still believes in vampires.

They say that for every slayer that dies, three are born, but in modern times usually only one accepts the calling. Even those numbers dwindle after some time because slayers will rethink their vocation and quit. Those who do accept their calling and stick with it are still registered, believe it or not, through the headquarters of the original slayer order, which is based in England.

Unlike Buffy Summers of television fame, slayers never work with a "Scooby gang" or even with other slayers. They work alone and are very secretive. No real vampire slayer ever tells people about their calling, the vampires contend, primarily to protect themselves and their loved ones. Just like vampires, they have the legal authorities to worry about, as well.

Humans will reportedly shy away from a slayer just as they will a real vampire. They supposedly feel the intensity of the slayers' obsession to hunt down evil and do away with it.

Vampire slayers supposedly know inherently when they are in the presence of a vampire. They can easily sense a hungry sanguinarian or any vampire that is up to no good. Psychic vampires are reportedly more difficult to detect.

Vampires respect slayers because no magical or supernatural force can stop them from doing what they have to do to fulfill their calling. Theirs is an inherited power that is only removable by death.

The traits of a vampire slayer have been well-preserved in the lineage of these mystical warriors. They supposedly enjoy the same superhuman stamina and strength that a vampire does. These powers are more likely to be evident during the adrenaline rush of a battle. Slayers are very focused and are obsessed with their calling. Because they are the workaholics of the supernatural world, you aren't likely to meet a slayer at a party.

Supernatural beings, both vampires and demons, have an uncanny way of running into their enemy. Slayers rarely even must seek them out – they just lay in wait. Unless there is heavy demon or vampire activity reported in a particular region, a slayer may perform some patrolling to keep things in check.

Slayers also possess the ability to fashion weapons out of virtually anything in their environment. If they bring a weapon with them at all, it will be a wooden stake, simply because they can pass through metal detectors and can be disposed of easily.

About the only thing that tips the scales into the vampire's favor is a slayer's arrogance. A vampire can kill a slayer if the slayer ignores his or her instincts in a no-win situation. Slayers are a very real threat to any vampire, even ones that are minding their own business.

Vampires also must watch out for "Vampire Hunters." Hunters aren't nearly as much of a threat as a slayer because they are just regular humans. Because they don't have the supernatural abilities of a Slayer, Hunters tend to work in packs and bring along heavy weaponry.

Identifying a Vampire

Traditionally, there were several ways to identify a vampire. Until the last few hundred years, it was common to open graves to examine corpses for decomposition. If the body hadn't decayed, the people believed it was a vampire. In Romania, villagers believed horses wouldn't cross the grave of a vampire, so they were often let loose in cemeteries to search for undead.

In those days, vampires were blamed for causing misfortunes like mysterious deaths, illness and plagues. Villagers grew nervous about the possibilities of vampires when their neighbors reported unexplained deaths, people becoming weak for no reason, when people reported dreams of vampire attacks, or if someone who recently died was reported to have been seen walking at night. *(The latter is a very common experience across many cultures – most likely due to the early psychological mourning process.)*

Villagers began digging up graves until they found a suspect. To find one, they'd look for holes in the ground above the grave. If found, men would open the coffin for further clues.

Evidence that a corpse belonged to a vampire included open eyes, ruddy complexion, no decay, long hair, long nails, bite marks on the neck, a shroud that was devoured, the presence of blood and flexible limbs. Pathologists today could explain many of these tell-tale signs away with the simple facts of early decomposition.

How to Not Become a Vampire

Did you know that, traditionally, being bitten by a vampire was far from the only way one might become one? It's true. Depending on the culture and era, a wide variety of means were thought to turn humans into vampires. Being bitten on the neck by a vampire is only the most common one, popularized by movies and books, and followed closely by drinking a vampire's blood.

Here are some not-so-commonly known legends about what needed to happen to turn a human into a vampire:

- Persuading your brother to walk in his sleep.
- Eating sheep that were killed by a werewolf.
- Stealing ropes used to lower coffins into the grave.
- Living an immoral life.
- Presiding over a Mass while in a state of mortal sin.
- Being born on a holy day.
- Being weaned too early
- Having a mother who was stared at by a vampire when she was pregnant with you. This unfortunate occurrence usually turned Mom into a vampire, too. Some traditions say that expectant fathers catching a vampire's eye could cause the same outcome.
- Having an abundance of hair at birth.
- Being born with teeth or a third nipple, or a variety of other birth defects or anomalies.
- Being illegitimate and having illegitimate parents.
- Dying at birth without being baptized.
- Being excommunicated or labeled a heretic by the Church.
- Committing suicide.
- Practicing black magic.
- Having a cat or another animal jump over your corpse before it is buried.

- ➢ Repeatedly lying to your parents.
- ➢ Being cursed by your parents.

It's pretty evident that if there was any truth in the legends of these methods, the world would be overrun by vampires. Many of these tall tales were created by the Christian church to keep parishioners in line with Biblical teaching and to create some order in society.

Killing a Vampire

REMINDER: It is our position that vampires are NOT real and do NOT require killing. The following is therefore for education and entertainment only! Some of these ideas may inspire safe, modern day actions you can take to "kill" Pigula and protect yourself from nighttime overeating. That is the sole reason we are presenting them here.

The list of legendary methods of killing vampires is almost as long as the ways to keep them at bay. The online vampire community insists that vampires today have human bodies and can be killed any way that any other human could be. Here are some of the traditional methods *(please remember this is just for illustration as a metaphor to help you stop overeating at night– do not under any circumstances attempt to actually execute these behaviors with any other person and/or animal, living, dead, and/or "undead")*:

- ➢ Stabbing a vampire in the heart with a wooden stake is probably the most well-known method of killing vampires. This method of slaying a vampire has been a legend for literally hundreds of years. Stakes are typically made of ash or aspen, which traditionally is the wood that made the cross on which Christ was crucified. To kill, the stake must penetrate the vampire's heart. In some communities during medieval times the stake was also often used in vampire prevention. Family members would stake their family members' corpses in their coffins to pin them inside.

➢ A consecrated bullet fired through a vampire's coffin will reportedly kill him. Stories tell of vampire hunters who used silver bullets to destroy vampires. The Serbs believed a silver coin with a cross carved into it, cut into quarters and loaded into a shotgun shell would destroy a vampire if he or she was struck by the shell.

➢ In addition to bullets, silver stakes, spears and daggers are purportedly useful in slowing down and killing vampires. Silver is considered to symbolize purity and has been used for protection against evil in virtually every culture in the world throughout history.

➢ Hundreds of years ago, silver was often melted down to form amulets, jewelry, bullets, daggers and religious symbols such as crucifixes. Legend has it that silver amulets and daggers can be placed into the ground above a vampire's grave to keep it from escaping. Silver nails driven into coffin lids were purported to do the same.

➢ Unlike in the movies, silver was not the protective metal against vampires. In most legends, iron was thought to ward off the undead. The folklore includes putting iron shades under the children's beds, wearing an iron nail or hanging pieces of metal around the house. Silver was said to be effective against werewolves that died and came back as vampires.

➢ Any running water, like rivers, lakes, streams, was believed to protect humans in some vampire legends. Many people believed that vampires cannot cross running water.

➢ Beheading a vampire is a legendary mode of ending a vampire's reign of terror. In legend, vampires were beheaded, had their hearts staked and then cut out, their remains burned to ash and buried on consecrated grounds

➢ Sunlight -- Vampires are creatures of the night, living and feeding in darkness. **In medieval times though, sunlight did not kill vampires** – they move around during the day just like any human. In Bram Stoker's novel, *Dracula*, vampires could survive in the daytime, but without their strength and powers. **It's only been in the last 50 or 60 years that the new legend of sunlight frying vampires has emerged – primarily through the entertainment industry**. Pop culture, movies and novels have made sunlight the ultimate vampire killer.

➢ The online vampire community says that all vampires are sensitive to the sun. Although it can make them very uncomfortable, none have exploded into ash.

➢ Cremation or fire is another mythological method of killing a vampire. This reportedly works when the vampire's ashes are scattered or when the head and heart has been removed before the cremation. It evidently is important that the vampire be burned thoroughly, or it will come back seeking vengeance.

➢ Immersion in water was the way to go in legends in some parts of the world.

➢ Extracting the vampire's heart. Some legends say that boiling the heart in vinegar, wine or oil would do the trick.

APPENDIX C - THE 100 BEST VAMPIRE MOVIES OF ALL TIME

What follows is an admittedly subjective list of the 100 greatest vampire movies of all time, listed in chronological order. If the vampire metaphor has been helpful to you, you may wish to watch them to strengthen your understanding and spot patterns which may enhance your resolve.

1. Les Vampires (1915)

Irma Vep stalks Paris in a seven-hour epic that scores high on style and set

the look for vampire femme-fetales to come

2. Drakula (1921)

Rumored to be brilliant, but sadly no copies remain in existence

3. Nosferatu (1922)

A little-known German actor Max Schreck as Count Orlock...a thinly veiled

Dracula movie, and still one of the scariest yet. There are dozens of versions of this movie. My favorite was the one with the "Symphony of Horrors" soundtrack appended. *(The original movie was silent).*

4. London After Midnight (1927)

Lon Chaney is a vampire in human disguise. The first full-length vampire

feature movie, it is based on a short story. "The Hypnotist" by director Tod

Browning

5. Dracula (1931)

Bela Lugosi defines Dracula for decades to come. Both the accent and his balletic style of movement bring real power and menace.

6. Vampyr (1932)

A loose adaptation of Sheridan Le Fanu's classic story Carmilla, a young man,

David Gray comes up against Margueritte Chopin, an elderly female vampire

7. The Vampire Bat (1933)

Lionel Atwill plays a mad scientist Dr. Otto Nieman who fakes several

Vampire-like deaths to obtain blood to feed the creature he has created.

8 Mark of the Vampire (1935)

Tod Browning's sound remake of his original London After Midnight. It was also

released as Werewolf of Paris and The Vampire of Prague. Bela Lugosi once more as the vampire.

9 Condemned to Live (1935)

Prof. Paul Kristan is "condemned to live" after being turned into a vampire by

the full moon. He then unwillingly begins attacking the residents of a small

European village.

10. Dracula's Daughter (1936)

A sequel to Dracula, based on Bram Stoker's short story "Dracula's Guest" and

the first feature film centered on a female vampire

11. The Return of Dr. X (1939)

Humphrey Bogart is turned into a vampire by blood transfusions.

12. The Devil Bat (1940)

A mad scientist (Bela Lugosi again) creates giant vampire bats to set on his

perceived enemies. Also released as: Killer Bats and as Devil Bats.

13. Spooks Run Wild (1941)

Lugosi again, playing a stage magician who is suspected of being a vampire.

14. Son of Dracula (1943)

Lon Chaney, Jr. as Count Alucard emigrates to the States in search of a

bride.

15. Dead Men Walk (1943).

George Zucco portrays a vampire with a human twin brother. *(Also released as:*

Creatures of the Devil.)

16. The Return of the Vampire (1944).

Lugosi plays a vampire reanimated when his stake is removed in England during

World War II.

17. House of Frankenstein (1944)

A monster fest, with Dracula, Frankenstein's monster, the Wolf-man, and

Boris Karloff as a mad scientist. *(A short version was released as Doom of*

Dracula)

18. House of Dracula (1945)

John Carradine reprises his role as Dracula in a sequel to House of

Frankenstein

19 Crime Doctor's Courage (1945)

Dr. Ordway, criminal psychologist, investigates a dance team that is suspected

of being vampires.

20. Isle of the Dead (1945)

Boris Karloff as a military officer in a rural Eastern European village who

believes that a vampire is on the loose.

21. Valley of the Zombies (1945)

A diver returns from the dead but needs fresh blood to stay alive.

22. Face of Marble (1946)

John Carradine as a mad professor revives a dead dog which attacks people and

drinks their blood.

23. The Vampire's Ghost (1946)

A vampire causes panic in a small African village

24. The Devil Bat's Daughter (1946)

Sequel to "The Devil Bat". The daughter gets visited in her sleep.

25. Abbott and Costello Meet Frankenstein (1948)

Lugosi as Dracula attempts to steal Lou Costello's brain and place it in

Frankenstein's monster

26. Old Mother Riley Meets the Vampire (1948)

Lugosi crosses the Atlantic and does his Dracula stuff in a British comedy.

27. I, Vampiri (1957)

The French police discover the blood-drained bodies of young women floating in

the river Seine.

28. El Vampiro (1957)

An ancient vampire comes to Mexico to revive the body of his dead brother.

(Christopher Lee has said that Count Lavud, the vampire in this film, inspired

his portrayal of Hammer's Count Dracula)

29. El Ataud Del Vampiro (1957)

A sequel to El Vampiro. A vampire stalks the corridors of a hospital

30. The Vampire (1957)

A different take on the legend, the vampire is a shambling figure who can walk

in the sun, more like a drug addict, but addicted to blood.

31. Blood of Dracula (1957)

A schoolteacher's experiment turns young, beautiful girls into vampires at a

residential school.

32. Dracula (1958)

Christopher Lee's first outing as the Count for Hammer Films, and an

unforgettable ending in the dining hall of the chateau with Peter Cushing

swinging on the curtains. *(Also known as Horror of Dracula.)*

33. Blood of the Vampire (1958)

Sir Donald Wolfit plays a vampiric doctor brought back to life and seeking a

cure for his condition.

34. The Return of Dracula (1958)

Dracula, played by Francis Lederer, arrives in the USA and causes mayhem in a

quiet township

35. Curse of the Undead (1959)

Dracula goes West and terrorizes a small Western town in the first vampire

western.

36. Brides of Dracula (1960)

Hammer's second vampire movie. Cushing's Van Helsing tracks a vampire in a

girls' boarding school.

37. Blood and Roses (1961)

Roger Vadim's lesbian adaptation of Le Fanu's Carmilla *(Also known as "Et*

Mourir De Plaiser")

38. El Mundo de Los Vampiros (1961)

A vampire keeps a horde of sub-human vampires in a subterranean vault. *(Of course he does! I mean, who wouldn't?)*

39. Black Sunday (1961)

Barbara Steele is a vampire/witch in Mario Bava's masterpiece

40. La Invasion de Los Vampiros (1961)

Mysterious deaths occur on the night of the full moon near the Lagoon of Death

in a small 16th century village.

41. Kiss of the Vampire (1962)

A young couple stumbles upon a mysterious family of vampires and their demonic leader. A non-Dracula Hammer movie.

42. The Wurdalak (1963)

Boris Karloff's only part as a vampire as a father who preys on his own family

(Also known as "Black Sabbath")

43. The Last Man on Earth (1964)

Vincent Price is the last man alive in a planet of vampires after an atomic

holocaust. *(Based on Richard Matheson's classic novel "I am Legend")*

44. Billy the Kid vs Dracula (1965)

A reformed Billy the Kid has to stop Count Dracula from stealing his girlfriend

45. Dracula, Prince of Darkness (1965)

A group of tourists are killed off one by one to provide the fuel to reanimate

Christopher Lee as the Count in a Hammer film.

46. Devils of Darkness (1965)

A satanic cult in a modern-day French village protects an ancient leader of the

undead.

47. Planet of the Vampires (1965)

Italian sci-fi where the crew turn into space vampires. (Also known as Terrore

Nello Spazio)

48. Blood Bath (1966)

An artist believes that he is the reincarnation of a vampire, paints beautiful

girls and then kills them by dipping their bodies in vats of hot wax.

49. Theatre of Death (1966)

A Parisian theatre is the center of a series of ghastly murders.

50. The Fearless Vampire Killers (1967)

A pair of incompetent vampire hunters travel through the Transylvanian winter

in search of their prey. (Also known as "Dance of the Vampires")

51. A Taste of Blood (1967)

An American businessman drinks from a strange brandy bottle, and finds himself

turning into his ancestor, Count Dracula *(Also known as "The Secret of Dr*

Alucard")

52. Dracula Has Risen from the Grave (1968)

Christopher Lee goes after a Monseigneur's daughter in his third outing as the

Count

53. Taste the Blood of Dracula (1969)

Christopher Lee as the Count gives some Victorian gentlemen more thrills than

they bargained for.

54. Count Yorga, The Vampire (1970)

An East European count preys on the citizens of LA

55. Lust for a Vampire (1970)

An English schoolteacher in Transylvania falls victim to a vampire beauty

56. House of Dark Shadows (1970)

Barnabas Collins finds the reincarnation of an ancient lost love and vows to

make her his for eternity

57. The Vampire Lovers (1970)

Hammer's "Carmilla" adaptation. Peter Cushing is a father losing his daughter

to the attentions of a female vampire

58. The Scars of Dracula (1970)

Two innocent victims discover the drained corpse of their friend in Dracula's castle.

59. Countess Dracula (1970)

Ingrid Pitt plays Countess Dracula, a tyrant who kills for the blood to satisfy

her craving to remain young and beautiful

60. The Night Stalker (1971)

A reporter investigating a series of murders discovers the victims were all

drained of blood and has to convince the authorities that a vampire is on the

loose.

61. Dracula A.D. 1972 (1972)

Count Dracula (Christopher Lee) is reincarnated during a Black Mass, held by a

group of young people in swinging London.

62. Crypt of the Living Dead (1972)

A 700-year-old vampire is released to cause mayhem.

63. Dracula (1973)

Jack Palance as Dracula in a retelling of the original story

64 Captain Kronos, Vampire Hunter (1973)

After several victims are robbed of youth an expert swordsman gives chase to

the culprit.

65. Satanic Rites of Dracula (1973)

Christopher Lee as CEO of a multinational conglomerate germ warfare in a silly

tale of germ warfare and world domination.

66 Legend of the Seven Golden Vampires (1974)

Prof. Van Helsing (Peter Cushing) is up against seven rotting vampires clad in

gold masks in a vampire and kung fu extravaganza

67. Andy Warhol's Dracula (1974)

Italian/French co-production with aging Dracula and a bevvy of virginal

beauties.

68. Leonor (1975)

Buenel's take on the vampire legend as a nobleman dabbles with dark forces and

resurrects a vampire in place of his lost love

69. Dracula's Dog (1977)

Zoltan, Hound of Dracula heads for the USA in search of the count's last living

descendant *(Also known as Zoltan, Hound of Dracula).*

70. Martin (1977)

A study of a blood drinking obsessive who may, or may not, be the real thing.

71. Dracula (1979)

A fine cast, including Frank Langella and Laurence Olivier, ham it up in a

faithful retelling of the original story.

72. Nosferatu-The Vampire (1979)

Klaus Kinski makes a stunning Nosferatu in a slow but stylish retelling of the

1920's classic.

73. Love at First Bite (1979)

George Hamilton as an urbane, witty count with all the best lines in a modern

spoof.

74. Salem's Lot: The Movie (1979)

Originally a 4-hour tv movie, this is a cut down version, but still packs a

punch, especially when the “vampirised” kid raps on the window outside.

75. The Hunger (1983)

Stylish vampires-as-yuppies flick with a stunning pair of vamps in Catherine

Deneuve and David Bowie.

76. Fright Night (1985)

A "My neighbor is a vampire" flick. Lots of fun, and plenty of homages to old

movies of the past.

77. Lifeforce (1985)

A space expedition brings back a naked female space vampire to demolish London. Hokum played straight by a fine cast of British character actors.

78 Once Bitten (1985)

An ancient countess needs the blood of young male virgins to keep her alive.

79. Vamp (1986)

Grace Jones as a stunning vampiress chases three college students through a

nightmare world around the "After Dark" club.

80. The Lost Boys (1987)

MTV generation vamps terrorize a sea-side town armed with perfect teeth and a

nice line in one-liners.

81. The Monster Squad (1987)

A team of vampire hunters try to stop Dracula taking over a small American town

82. Near Dark (1987)

A modern-day cowboy is taken by a pack of roaming vamps in a stylish modern

western.

83. Vampire's Kiss (1989)

Nicholas Cage's girlfriend gives him reason to be paranoid when she leaves her

mark on his neck.

84 I Bought a Vampire Motorcycle (1990)

Comic British blokes find their motorbike runs on blood, not petrol.

85. Bram Stroker's Dracula (1992)

High gloss, high budget romanticized version of the original story.

86. Innocent Blood (1992)

John Landis turns to vampires, and the sexiest vamp ever has a brush

with the Mafia.

87. Buffy, the Vampire Slayer (1992)

Teenage angst and high kicking high school stunts that started a phenomenon

88. Interview with the Vampire (1994)

Sumptuous look at Anne Rice's classic, as Brad Pitt tells his two

hundred-year history.

89. Vampire in Brooklyn (1995)

Wes Craven directs Eddie Murphy in a great mix of horror and comedy

90. Dracula: Dead and Loving It (1995)

Mel Brooks turns his attention to Dracula with all the subtlety you would expect.

91. Addicted to Murder (1995)

Serial killer and vampire form an unholy pact.

92. From Dusk 'Till Dawn (1996)

Tarantino and Clooney think they've escaped the law, but they choose

the wrong bar in which to wind down. And the stunning table dancer is

more than she seems.

93. The Night Flyer (1997)

Stephen Kings tale of a vampire who takes advantage of technology and

stalks small airports from the sky.

94. Blade (1998)

Wesley Snipes is mean moody and magnificent in the comic book here

brought to life story of the vengeful vamp who can walk in the day.

95. John Carpenter's Vampires (1998)

The Vatican's vampire hit squad meets an ancient foe who is stronger

than any they have ever encountered.

96. Shadow of the Vampire (2000)

In a telling of the story of the making of the film, the actor who

played the 1922 Nosferatu, Max Schreck, is a real vampire.

97 Jesus Christ, Vampire Hunter (2001)

After the second coming, JC has to cope with an infestation of vamps

in a gloriously daft mixture of prophecy, kung fu and horror.

98. Blade II (2002)

Wesley Snipes reprises his role, with more swordplay, high kicking and daring do

99. Qian Ji Bian (2003)

Honk Kong high kicks and vampire hunting thrills in a slam bang action movie.

100 Underworld (2003)

Vampires versus werewolves in gothic high-tech fantasy that's both stylish and fun

APPENDIX D - WHERE DO ZOMBIES COME FROM?

Just in case you weren't convinced of the human mind's capacity to develop and embrace false beliefs, we thought we'd illustrate with another frightening creature rampant in cultural myth... The Zombie!

Picture yourself all alone and stranded in your car on the side of a deserted country road. Your cellular phone is dead. Your gas tank is empty. You're miles from the nearest home, gas station, or telephone.

And the worst part?

As the sun has started going down, you start glimpsing movement to your right in the field, but you dismiss it as your imagination and focus on the road. Surely, a pair of headlights will appear in the gloom to rescue you.

You hear a noise! The sound of twigs being cracked and broken under heavy footsteps! Was someone coming?!

Slowly, you turn toward the sound and see a man approaching. Your heart suddenly is overflowing with relief; you've been saved!

You rush toward him, smiling and waving your hands in welcome. Then, you stop because as you've gotten closer, you realize that there's something not quite right about this man.

His movement is slow and sporadic. He seems to be dragging his left leg behind him, and it seems to be strangely distorted as if it were badly broken and had never healed properly. His clothes seem about twenty years out of fashion, and his face seems to be missing clumps of flesh.

He reaches out his arm toward you, and his mouth begins to move in an awkward way as if he's trying to speak but has forgotten how. You start backing up slowly; you don't want to startle him.

You back up a little further, a little further, a little further. The man's grayish green hand is only inches from you and now you can clearly see that one of his eyes is missing. You look away from the horrid face but not before noticing the thousands of squirming white maggots that now call the abandoned eye socket home.

You back up further and bump into something cold. With relief, you think it's just your car and you turn to jump inside where you can lock the doors, roll up all the windows, and pray for rescue.

But then you realize that your car is still 8 feet away and behind you is another man similar in many ways to the one now in front you. Only this one can talk . . . and his ghoulish black lips move and form one word as his arms tighten around your shaking body: “Brains!”

Just then, a car passes by on the road and stops when they see the abandoned car. The driver thinks about getting out, but then hears a sudden, horrified scream and screeches away while telling himself it was all just a dream.

Thankfully for you, none of this was real. After all, zombies are just figments of our imagination, right? They don't exist anymore than witches, vampires, or werewolves, do they?

What if you’re wrong? What if that scratching sound on your window just now wasn't a tree branch or a neighbor cat? What if it was actually a monster that has been the star of dozens of fright flicks over the last 7 decades? What if it was really a creature that isn't based solely on human imagination but that had its origins in something very real and very terrifying? What if not everything you've seen or read about the undead was a lie?

Then, you'd better bolt your windows, lock your doors, and stay with me as I lead you on a journey that will take you closer to the truth about zombies than you ever dared to go.

Zombie Reality

Zombies ARE an actual phenomenon that has been documented by researchers, but the truth is that real zombies have little in common with their big screen counterparts.

Haitian Zombies

The Western World first became truly fascinated with zombies during the American occupation of Haiti between 1915 and 1934. Soldiers and other Americans heard tales of the dead coming back to life as creatures that could walk, talk, and eat but which had few memories or cognitive skills.

According to these stories, the cause of these "living dead" is the bokor, or voodoo witch doctor. While it may sound like the back story for a big budget feature film, it is very real, but to understand zombies, one must first have some knowledge of voodoo.

Voodoo is a religion which has its roots in Haiti and the nearby Caribbean islands, but which is today practiced by over 50 million people around the world. Obviously, the largest portion of those practitioners are still based in Haiti, but you can also find some in major U. S. cities, such as New Orleans, Los Angeles, Houston, and Charleston.

Voodoo was actually brought to America as a result of the slave trade, and many slaves continued to practice their religion as a way of dealing with their captivity. Their white masters were at first curious about the strange new belief system, but they eventually began to severely punish their slaves who maintained their spiritual practices. In fact, many slaves were mutilated and even buried alive for simply possessing a fetish, which is any symbol of a god or spirit that is believed to connect the mortal to the divine. Most slaves were baptized quickly as a way to stop the spread of their "unnatural" religion.

In Haiti, Voodoo revolves around the worship of a large pantheon of gods, including the spirits of respected ancestors. Worshipers do believe in a supreme god, known as Gran Met, who is credited with the creation of the universe, but he is not the one who is most actively followed. Actually, Voodoo has two main gods: Danbhala-Wedo (the Grand Serpent) and Aida-Wedo (the Rainbow). These two gods, who are also believed to be man and wife, are believed to have brought the knowledge of procreation and of spiritual wisdom to humans.

Another important figure in Voodoo is Legha. Legha opens the door between the mortal world and the spiritual world so that humans can communicate with their gods. Many worshipers identify Legha with St. Peter or with Jesus Christ because in many places the ancient practices of Voodoo have been blended with Christianity.

Magic and sorcery are important elements of Voodoo as well. Healers and diviners, known as houngan and mambo, are considered spiritual leaders. They use their skills to help both the living and the dead. For example, during one type of ceremony, dead spirits are allowed to enter and take over the bodies of the living so that they can complete any unfulfilled business in the mortal realm.

The bokor is also a magic practitioner, but he is more interested in the black arts than in those of healing. However, the bokor is never viewed as evil. Voodoo believers see evil as a mirror image of what is good. It is neither better nor worse; it is just different. They also realize that evil is necessary in the world to maintain balance.

The bokor is the one responsible for creating zombies. But how do they do it?

The process of zombification is not as complex as you might believe. In fact, you could probably do it yourself if you had the right ingredients, which include some exotic plants, a few worms and lizards, a little bit of human flesh, and a number of other items that would give the average person the willies. But the most important ingredient is the puffer fish, a Japanese delicacy that is most often found in sushi.

What's so special about the puffer fish, you might ask. Well, the answer is that it's incredibly toxic. The fish contains a lethal poison known as tetrodotoxin which is highly concentrated in the liver, sex organs, skin, and bones of the fish. In small amounts, tetrodotoxin is not harmful but it does make the person feel a bit "high."

In large amounts, however, the chemical causes paralysis, an extreme reduction in body function, and eventually death.

Additionally, many bokors use the skin of a poison toad. The toad's poison causes muscle relaxation and decreased respiratory function.

Bokors combine all of the ingredients and give it to a person whom they have selected for zombification. Sometimes they will choose someone who is on the verge of death, but often victims are perfectly healthy individuals.

The tetrodotoxin (either alone or with the toad's poison) works fast. The victim's heartbeat and respiration slow so much that it would barely be detectable. The person is also in a state of paralysis so they cannot move or communicate, even though most remain completely conscious and alert during the entire ordeal. To any untrained eye, the person would seem to be dead, and they are usually buried rapidly. Yes, they are buried while they are still technically alive.

After their burial, the bokor will dig up the body and use another magic powder to revive them partially. The intense trauma of being buried alive while still lucid causes many victims to lose their memories and to become little more than mindless robots who do whatever the bokor asks. After all, they have seen his power and know that he must be obeyed. Plus, some bokors supposedly administer an antidote to their victims which is made from the jimsonweed plant (also known as Jamestown weed, mad apple, and moon flower) and which causes memory loss.

There have been numerous documented encounters with zombies in Haiti over the years. One young man from Port-au-Prince who was stabbed during a robbery appeared six months later at his parents' home. He told them that a bokor had stolen his body while it was en route to the hospital after the crime and how the bokor had turned him into a zombie. While he was somewhat normal for a while, he eventually stopped communicating and died soon after. Another zombie sighting was reported by writer Stephen Bonsal back in 1912. He described participating in the funeral of a man who had died from a high fever. According to Mystica.com, "Some days later the supposedly dead man was found dressed in grave clothes, tied to a tree, moaning. The poor wretch soon recovered his voice but not his mind. He was identified by his wife, by the physician who had pronounced him dead, and by the clergyman. The victim recognized no-one, and his days were spent moaning inarticulate words no-one could understand."

Haiti certainly took these reports and the continuing fear of its citizens over potential zombification seriously. Article 249 of the Haitian penal code states, "It shall also be qualified as attempted murder the employment which may be made against any person of substances which, without causing actual death, produce a lethargic coma more or less prolonged. If, after the person had been buried, the act shall be considered murder no matter what result follows." So, you should be very careful about trying to work your zombie magic in Haiti, or you might end up charged with murder.

Buried . . . But Not Quite Dead

Of course, Haiti can't be given all the credit for the creation of the zombie mythos. Westerners have long believed that people could come back from the dead, and they had good reasons for those beliefs: they'd seen it firsthand, or so they thought.

Many of the so-called "undead" that have been reported throughout history were never really "dead" to begin with. Most of them, like their Haitian counterparts, endured the horror of being buried alive! The only difference was that there were no bokors or magic powders at work for most of these unfortunate individuals.

Before embalming (the process by which a body is drained of blood and replaced with chemicals that slow the decaying process), the time between death and burial had to be quick. For one, the bodies decayed very quickly, particularly in the summer and needed to be disposed of before that happened. For another, contact with the dead could also spread disease and attracted vermin (such as rats). Since there wasn't much time to wait, many people who were simply comatose or who were paralyzed in some way ended up in the ground even though they were not dead.

How common was this experience? In the late 19th century, bodies were moved from the Fort Randall Cemetery and the overseer of the procedures reported that at least 2% of the bodies showed signs that they had been buried alive. During the 17th century, one researcher reported the following findings:

- Almost 220 cases of individuals who barely escaped being buried alive.
- Just under 150 cases of someone being actually buried alive.
- 10 cases of a victim being dissected before they were medically dead
- 2 people who were found to be alive after the embalming process has been started.

So how do these unfortunate cases lead up to a belief in the undead?

Let's look at some actual cases. In the 1850's, a young girl suddenly died from diphtheria in South Carolina and her body was quickly placed inside a mausoleum to prevent her disease from spreading. A few years later, the mausoleum was opened for another funeral and behind the door, the mourners discovered the small skeleton of the girl who had obviously awoken in the tomb and tried to escape without success.

What would you think if you saw such a thing? Would it truly be a difficult leap in thought to assume that she had come back from the dead but had been unable to get out of the mausoleum?

About 100 years before that incident, a professor at Halle University was provided with a late-night delivery of a criminal's body. He'd just been hung his body was to be used for medical dissections. The body was left in its bag while the exhausted professor retired for the night. A few hours later, he awoke and found the man standing naked in his bedroom holding the now empty sack.

How would you rationalize such a horrifying discovery, especially if you trusted the medical establishment of your times?

Of course, incidents of the "dead" coming back to life is not reserved for only past centuries. The following events were reported in a news story from 1993:

Sipho William Mdletshe might as well be dead, as far as his fiancée is concerned.

Declared deceased after a traffic accident in Johannesburg, South Africa, Mdletshe, 24, spent two days in a metal box in a mortuary before his cries alerted workers, who rescued him.

But Mdletshe is heartbroken, because his fiancée, who also was hurt in the crash, doesn't believe his story and refuses to see him. She thinks he's a zombie who returned from the dead to haunt her.

Obviously, Mdletshe's finance believed more strongly in the idea of zombies than she did in the possibility that doctors might have made a mistake by declaring her beloved dead.

These real tales of unfortunate people being buried alive were passed on through generations and became a part of our urban legends. One example is the story of Marjorie Elphinstone who was buried in Scotland and whose grave was robbed soon after. While the robbers tried to pry loose the jewelry from her body, she groaned loudly. They fled in terror, and she returned to her husband and lived with him until he died six years before she finally passed away for real.

While none of these people were actually zombies, it shouldn't be hard to understand how coming face to face with someone whose funeral you had attended might make you feel a little jumpy, especially if you take into consideration that the victims in these cases would probably never be quite the same after surviving such an ordeal.

Events in the absence of appropriate information to explain them results in false beliefs which, once they've taken hold, can run wild in both the mind and the populace at large.

APPENDIX E – HOW TO STOP HATING YOURSELF FOR NIGHTTIME OVEREATING MISTAKES

Most nighttime overeaters suffer with severe self-castigation after a mistake. Pigula tries its best to beat them down and make them feel too weak to resist the next binge. This is a piercing insight, and often sufficient to help many people soften the crushing self-loathing and get on with recovering. "Commit with perfection but forgive yourself with dignity" is the mantra we teach.

Moreover, Glenn is famous for telling people they do NOT have to deal with the emotional component of their overeating problem in order to get better. He explains that emotional issues do not cause overeating but are merely associated with it. There's always the voice of justification which makes it "OK" to overeat after you've created your best laid plans and sworn to follow a particular Food Rule.

See, before you cross the line, no matter how you're feeling inside, there's that little voice that says "Go ahead, it's OK because_____________"...and if you can just learn how to neutralize and/or ignore that little voice the overeating problem disappears. Stop justifying overeating no matter how you feel, and you won't overeat.

For this reason, it's entirely possible to hate yourself and still Never Binge Again. You do not have to fix the self-hatred in order to stop overeating at night. We stand by this position 100%

But notwithstanding the above, the emotions we endure can still be VERY uncomfortable, and if you allow them to run rampant you can, in fact, begin to feel too weak to resist. Feelings are NOT facts, and you never ARE too weak, but it's very unpleasant. And as a practical matter many people DO use self-critical thoughts and self-loathing feelings to justify the next binge.

For this reason, sometimes a deeper understanding of the emotional component of binge eating can help to drain a lot of the energy from these feelings and make them more bearable. Therefore, we've included this appendix in which we'll give you a very practical example of self-loathing, and how you might analyze the thoughts and emotions to neutralize their power.

Margaret was an old client of ours who's name and details have been changed to protect the innocent. In this session, Glenn was trying to help her let go of self-loathing associated with a recent bout of overeating. Please keep in mind this session was conducted years before Glenn fully articulated the principles in Never Binge Again. We call this session "Three Jelly Donuts and a Bagel."

THREE JELLY DONUTS AND A BAGEL

Most mornings "Margaret" found herself eating three jelly donuts and a buttered salt bagel. She didn't enjoy more than the first donut and the first few bites of the bagel, yet she always ate both donuts and every last crumb of the bagel. After each of these "meals" she would be very angry with herself and would call herself a "cow" or a "stupid idiot with no willpower." Sometimes she even told herself that she deserved to be fat and feel sluggish all day.

This routine had gone on for a few years prior to our work together. One day she came to our session complaining of having "done it again."

Here's how I began to help her become intrigued:

- ➢ **Margaret**: I'm such a moron. Every morning I tell myself I'm just going to have egg whites and oatmeal, which should be plenty to eat, but then I find myself back in the cafeteria getting my donuts and bagels. Every morning! I swear sometimes I think someone should just shoot me and get it over with. What the hell is wrong with me, I mean, don't you think I'd learn? I got A's and B's in college, why am I such a *$#@!*$#@! moron around food?" *(She then paused, waiting for me to react).*

- ➢ **Glenn**: I'm sorry, what kind of a moron did you say you were?

- ➢ **Margaret**: *(Laughs, then looks mad, then laughs again)* ... A *$#@!*$#@! moron, that's what I said! I am a jelly donut shoving, buttered bagel eating, *$#@!*$#@! moron!!! Is that what you wanted to know?

- ➢ **Glenn**: Well ... yes, kind of, thanks for explaining" *(she laughs again).* Really what I wanted to know was if it helps you to call yourself that. Does it get you any closer to your goal of eating egg whites and oatmeal in the morning?

- ➢ **Margaret**: Now I think YOU are a *$#@!*$#@! moron! *(laughs while saying this).*

- ➢ **Glenn**: Why?

- ➢ **Margaret**: *(Pauses, looks confused, then is silent, seems upset).*

- ➢ **Glenn**: It's OK, you can tell me why you think I'm a moron if you want. I'm curious about your thoughts.

- ➢ **Margaret**: *(a short silence, then says)* Actually, I know you're trying to get at something. It just seemed like a moronic question. Don't you think I'm a moron to eat like this all the time? I mean, don't you want to just smack yourself in the head when I leave and say, "I don't get it – why the hell does she eat this way all the time?" ... or don't you ever just want to shake me and say "snap out of it ... will you just stop eating the stupid donuts already for god's sake!??

➢ **Glenn**: No, that's not exactly how I feel.

➢ **Margaret**: *(laughs, then falls silent).*

➢ **Glenn**: Where did you go?

➢ **Margaret**: I was thinking that I was all stuck in the idea that one of us is a moron. Either I'm a moron for doing what I do every day with the stupid donuts or else you're a moron for not thinking I'm a moron. I'd rather that I was the moron than you because if you're the moron then I don't have much hope.

➢ **Glenn**: Why does one of us have to be a moron? What if neither of us were morons?

➢ **Margaret**: Well, what would we talk about then? *(semi-seriously).*

➢ **Glenn**: You feel as if we would have nothing to talk about if we were two smart people trying to figure out an eating problem you are having?

➢ **Margaret**: *(laughs)* Yes, I guess I do feel like that, or rather, I DID feel like that. It does make more sense to try to figure out the eating problem than to call myself a moron or call you a moron.

➢ **Glenn:** Good. Can I ask you a question about the eating problem then? Would it interest you to pursue that a little bit?

➢ **Margaret:** *(Looks a little relieved, and more focused)* Yes, actually, I'd like that.

➢ **Glenn:** I was curious to understand what you might have been feeling or thinking BEFORE you went to the cafeteria to buy the donuts and bagel.

➢ **Margaret:** Well... it was about 45 minutes before my meeting with Cheryl *(her boss).* I had gone over the proposal we were working on and thought it was pretty much ready to go. I thought that she should be happy with the work I did on the graphs and charts and tables. She can put them right into the presentation, but for some reason I was very nervous about talking to her about it. Nervous, actually, is putting it mildly. I was panicked. I don't know why I get so panicked about talking to Cheryl, but I get like that every time. I'm a pretty confident person in so many areas of my life, but when I'm around her my heart beats faster, I start to sweat a little bit... sometimes I actually have trouble speaking. Actually, now that I think about it, I feel like a moron around her.

➢ **Glenn**: So, you were feeling like a moron BEFORE you went to eat the donuts and buttered bagel? That's interesting.

➢ **Margaret**: (Emphatically) Yes, VERY interesting!" .... "What does that mean?

➢ **Glenn**: I'm not sure yet. Can you tell me more about your relationship with Cheryl? What is it about her that makes you feel inferior?

➢ **Margaret**: Cheryl is a very together person. She usually has the answers to anything someone asks her right at her fingertips. She dresses really sharply, she doesn't seem to have food problems, she's very pretty, she's married... she's kind of got what she wants in life – a very successful person.

➢ **Glenn**: You feel that your life is not together the way Cheryl's is?

➢ **Margaret**: Well, practically no one's life is really as together as her life is, except maybe my sister's, but particularly not mine.

➢ **Glenn**: It's interesting that you mention your sister. Did you also feel inferior around her?

➢ **Margaret**: Yes, absolutely. I was just as pretty for a while when I was thin, but she managed to maintain it, got married early, had two great kids, and now she has a much better job than mine. I absolutely feel inferior around her *(pauses)*.

➢ **Glenn**: So what's really interesting is that just before you felt compelled to go eat the donuts and the bagel, you were thinking about someone who reminded you of your sister. I'd be really curious ... and maybe you can think about this and talk to me more about it next time ... I'd be really curious to learn more about why you feel inferior next to your sister. I'd also be interested to learn about all the ways that Cheryl reminds you of your sister, PLUS some of the ways that the two of them are different.

➢ **Margaret**: I had no idea I would talk about this when I came in today. All I could think about was what a *$#@!*$#@! moron I was for eating the donuts and the bagel. This is really interesting.

➢ **Glenn**: It's brave of you to go beyond calling yourself a moron.

➢ **Margaret**: Maybe, and I'm interested to see where this leads me, but I still reserve the right to call one of us a moron if I want to.

➢ **Glenn**: As if I could really take that away from you! I'll see you next week.

➢ **Margaret**: *(walks out, smiling)*

DISCUSSION OF THREE JELLY DONUTS AND A BAGEL

Initially, Margaret's self-critical attitude actually served to help perpetuate the problem behavior. As long as she was intent on calling herself a moron, she was more interested in continuing to act on the thoughts and feelings which made her feel inadequate by eating two jelly donuts and a buttered bagel. If Margaret were to come to me today, I'd first help her develop specific rules and to identify the specific Pigula Whisper which made it possible for these feelings to jump into behavior and show her how to dispute these Squeals. Thereafter, I'd still try to get Margaret more intrigued about how harsh she was being to herself and actively try to soften this attitude. I'd point out this was the Pigula's way of getting her to feel too weak to resist the NEXT Binge. But twenty years ago, I didn't have these techniques in my arsenal, so I worked harder to understand the psychodynamics underlying the very harsh thoughts and feelings.

Developing a sense of intrigue with Margaret first involved gently calling attention to the self-critical behavior, without implying anything positive or negative about it. See, when someone is prone to self-criticism, they are prone to criticize themselves for criticizing themselves if you give them the opportunity! I avoided attempting to eliminate the self-critical thoughts right away, because I wanted to understand them first.

Rather than telling her "don't be ridiculous, you're not a moron, and certainly not a *$#@!*$#@! moron," I chose simply to draw her attention to the self-criticism, and in particular to the most aggressive part of her self-communication. *"I'm sorry, what kind of a moron did you say you were?"*

As is frequently the case, the above exploration with Margaret led to the insight that the self-critical feelings originated BEFORE the problem food behavior. In addition to "getting her high" with the all the sugar, starch and fat in her chosen Slop, eating poorly served to distract Margaret from experiencing the uncomfortable feelings of inferiority she had in her boss' presence. On a deeper level it distracted her from the same set of feelings she carried regarding her relationship with her sister.

Margaret became intrigued when she realized she possibly wasn't feeling inferior due to having eaten poorly, but rather her feelings of inferiority might have preceded her eating difficulty. This realization was intriguing because it offered hope. She could see that by examining the source of these feelings, she might find that she was indeed not inferior *(or at the very least she could identify specific areas of weakness and a specific plan to improve)*, whereas when she identified the problem in the jelly donuts there seemed to be little hope.

Finally, it's important to note her parting comments. Margaret "reserved the right" to call one of us a moron because she had not yet fully explored or understood the set of feelings which were so uncomfortable for her, and as such could not expect herself to immediately abandon her old ways. Today I'd understand and interpret this as more Pigula Whisper, but back then I felt softening self-criticism always meant being willing to pause and dig a little deeper when you discovered it.

Last, in order to overcome self-critical thoughts and feelings, one might ask what, exactly, they believe is the opposite. I believe the opposite of self-criticism is NOT self-praise, but INTRIGUE.

Perhaps the best way to illustrate the difference between intrigue and self-criticism is to talk about the differences between constructive confrontation, which is useful for many things in life, including sticking to a food plan for life, and criticism, which isn't good for much at all). Though we are ultimately most interested in the attitude we have towards ourselves – it is easiest to illustrate via attitudes we have in relationships, nowhere more apparent than in a couple's relationship.

In my thirties I did a LOT of couples' work. In fact, I saw over 200 couples, only two of whom ever got divorced to my knowledge! It was in this work that I first discovered people with weight problems are frequently quite confused about the concept of constructive confrontation. I'd frequently observe the obese person's spouse berate them, and when I tried to intervene to defuse or soften the situation, I invariably got some version of the following from the overweight individual: "Oh, Doc, he's just trying to help. I can take a little constructive criticism."

I believe in this way the overweight person had become a co-conspirator in their own oppression! Most people gloss over this concept, so please read that sentence again, because this is exactly what Pigula wants you to do by berating yourself after a mistake!

It seems the reasoning goes something like this:

- There is a need in all relationships for each partner to communicate dissatisfaction, otherwise nothing can be done about the problem.

- My partner is attempting to communicate his/her dissatisfaction.

- I should therefore just grin and bear it.

Indeed, there is something inherently appealing about this logic, and for certain, to have a successful relationship there are times when one needs to develop the ability to grin and bear. But in and of itself, this line of reasoning does NOT define constructive confrontation, because it omits THREE key elements which are necessary to achieve a constructive outcome:

- **RESPECT:** Constructive confrontations are communicated with respect for the listener. They target specific behaviors rather than the person as a whole. "If you weren't such a fatty you might fit into that dress" is NOT a constructive confrontation.

- **DIRECTION**: What makes a confrontation "constructive" is the provision of an alternate means of behavior ... a way to improve the situation. Otherwise, the listener is left only with negative feelings and no direction for improvement. "I hate when you make meatloaf on Saturdays. How many times do I have to tell you not to make *$#(@! meatloaf on Saturdays!!!" is NOT a constructive confrontation because it does NOT provide information about what the speaker DOES want for dinner.

- **MINIMUM NECESSARY FORCE**: Constructive confrontation uses the minimum amount of intensity required to get the listener's attention. There's no reason to escalate volume, hurl character accusations or to use other forms of negativity.

It is only when a confrontation is communicated with respect for the listener, when it targets a specific problem behavior and provides clear direction for how to improve the situation, and when it is communicated with the minimum force necessary to get the listener's full attention, that it can be considered constructive.

Taken in this context, I'm sure you'll see Pigula's pounding of the gavel in harsh judgment after your mistakes is anything but constructive!

The problem is, because the vast majority of the populace confuses the simple expression of thoughts and feelings for constructive communication, we have internalized and accepted self-critical attitudes. Almost nobody understands the elements of constructive communication reviewed above.

The confusion over constructive confrontation vs. destructive criticism has a serious implication for our internal psyches. Many of us *(especially those with weight issues)* have come to believe that it is constructive to endure negative communications from others about our weight, regardless of how they are communicated.

More importantly (and THIS is the point) ... **we have learned to talk to ourselves in the same harsh and directionless way!** When we see ourselves doing something wrong, we are just as harsh in the way we talk to ourselves as we have become accustomed to being talked to. We berate ourselves, rather than kindly, gently, and constructively confront those issues on which we need to work.

Is it any wonder, then, that we get stuck in self-loathing until we feel too weak to do anything but Binge?

AN ATTITUDE OF "INTRIGUE" IS THE SOLUTION

There are several aspects of intrigue that relieve our overdeveloped tendency to self-criticize:

- **TOLERANCE:** When we are intrigued, we are more willing to observe and examine alternatives with an open mind before demanding successful action.

- **ACKNOWLEDGING COMPLEXITY:** Most long-term problems are more complex than they seem on the surface. Being intrigued, by its very nature, implies an acknowledgement of the complexity of a situation. Indeed, the willingness to study a problem implies the understanding that there is more to it than meets the eye.

- **INTEREST IN THE BEST SOLUTION:** When we're harshly critical of ourselves, we focus on only the tip of the iceberg, and tend to look for a "quick fix" solution. On the other hand, when we're committed to finding a truly better solution, we first must give ourselves permission to slow down, study all the options and make a well-thought out decision that addresses ALL of the underlying issues. In other words, becoming intrigued not only forces us to be kind to ourselves, but it also sets us up to find a solution which addresses the problem much more comprehensively, possibly for the long term. As we find value in these solutions, we become more and more willing to look inward.

In contrast, when we're self-critical, not only do we make it nearly impossible to look inward but we also prevent ourselves from discovering true solutions to our food difficulties. In a way, one could say that being self-critical is actually a clever way of permitting us to continue eating poorly AND punishing ourselves for it at the same time. It's a weird way of beating yourself up for the NEXT binge. Like doing penance in advance.

In any case, you don't have to study all this too hard and I don't need to turn you into a psychologist to help you stop overeating at night. But if you find it difficult to let go of the self-loathing after a mistake, come back to these points please and briefly review them. Because if you can start to understand and expect constructive communication in all your affairs, you'll have a much easier time talking to yourself in the same light.

Now...

You. Go. Nail Pigula in its Coffin for good!

---

[1] This philosophy was first quoted in the 1949 movie "Knock on Any Door" by actor John Derek. The full quote was "Live fast, die young, and leave a good-looking corpse"

[Y1]BEST DISCLAIMER EVER

Made in the USA
Columbia, SC
24 July 2020

14605547R00126